100

HIEROGLYPHS

Think Like an Egyptian

BARRY KEMP

Granta Books

London

Granta Publications, 2/3 Hanover Yard,
Noel Road, London N1 8BE

First published in Great Britain by
Granta Books 2005

1 3 5 7 9 10 8 6 4 2

ISBN 1 86207 658 8

Hieroglyphic font by Barry Kemp

Typeset by M Rules

Printed and bound in Great Britain by
William Clowes Limited, Beccles, Suffolk

CONTENTS

ACKNOWLEDGEMENTS

The idea for this book came from the fertile mind of George Miller; the carving of my unwieldy English into something more readable and accurate was the task of Bella Shand, both of them of Granta Books. Andy Boyce drew the hieroglyphs.

TIMELINE

Dates for the earlier periods of ancient Egyptian history are still not settled, although the margins of variation are mostly within decades. The dates cited here are those of *The Oxford History of Ancient Egypt*, edited by Ian Shaw (Oxford 2000).

Predynastic periods (Neolithic)	c. 5300–3000 BC
Early Dynastic Period (Dyns. 1–2) (or Archaic Period)	c. 3000–2686 BC
Old Kingdom (Dyns. 3–8)	2686–2160 BC
1st Intermediate Period (Dyns. 9–mid-11)	2160–2055 BC
Middle Kingdom (Dyns. mid-11–13/14)	2055–1650 BC
2nd Intermediate Period (Dyns. 15–17) (includes the Palestinian 'Hyksos' Dynasty in the north of Egypt)	1650–1550 BC
New Kingdom (Dyns. 18–20)	1550–1069 BC
3rd Intermediate Period (Dyns. 21–24)	1069–715 BC
Late Period	715–332 BC
Kushite (Sudanese)/Assyrian rule (Dyn. 25)	747–656 BC
Saite Period (Dyn. 26)	664–525 BC
1st Persian Period (Dyn. 27)	525–359 BC
Local dynasties (Dyn. 28–30)	359–343 BC
2nd Persian Period ('Dyn. 31')	343–332 BC
Conquest by Alexander the Great	332 BC
Ptolemaic Period	332–30 BC
Death of Queen Cleopatra VII	30 BC
Roman Period	30 BC–AD 395
Egypt ruled from Byzantium (Constantinople or Istanbul)	AD 395–642
Arab conquest of Egypt	AD 642

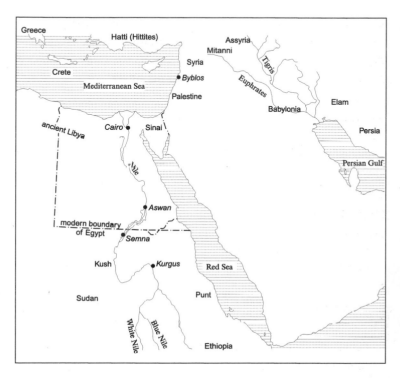

Map 1. The Middle East

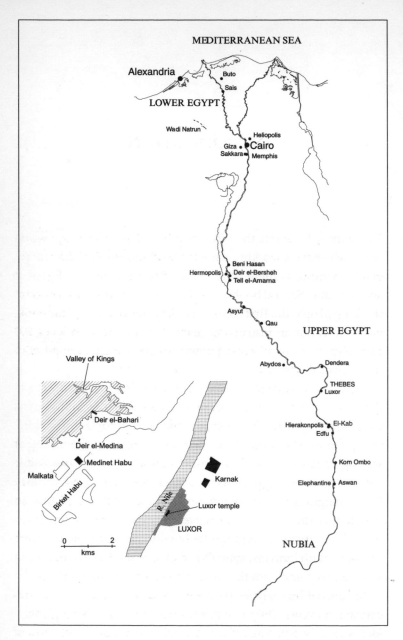

Map 2. Egypt

INTRODUCTION

There must be about the same number of people in the world today who have a working knowledge of ancient Egyptian hieroglyphic writing as there were literate people in ancient Egypt at any one time. Several books published in recent years are aimed at teaching people the first steps in reading hieroglyphs. This book, however, is not an instruction manual; rather, it introduces 100 hieroglyphs as a set of entry points into the world and mindset of the ancient Egyptians.

Egyptian hieroglyphs are one of the earliest recorded steps in the creation of the written word, a remarkable invention central to the development of a complex society. Hieroglyphic writing uses pictures, like some other early scripts, inviting the view that writing began as a codified artistic representation of the visible world. Scenes on Egyptian tomb and temple walls of, say, country life or religious rituals sometimes integrate text and picture so closely that the whole scene is like an enlarged hieroglyph, particularly as artistic conventions for hieroglyphs and drawings were the same, with humans, animals and objects rendered in outline in a precise way, and with the rules of perspective often ignored.

Streams of hieroglyphs are not like a piece of cinefilm or a strip cartoon, however. Only a relatively small number of hieroglyphs – ideographs – are pictures of the idea being communicated. Most of the signs require the instantaneous mental substitution of concepts that are quite different from the represented image – the sounds of letters, singly or in groups. They reveal a mental ability to override first impressions of what a picture 'stands for', and to construct instead a system of meaning with its own integrity. Hieroglyphic writing, just like all full writing systems, is the product of a highly sophisticated level of brain processing. There is nothing naïve about it.

Some phonetic signs express single sounds, like letters of an alphabet; others express two or three sounds. A more limited set of signs, known as determinatives, can be added to the end of a noun or verb to place that word into a more general category. A good example of a determinative is a pair of walking legs, ʌ, added to the end of verbs of motion. Hieroglyphic writing requires a constant shifting back and forth between symbol and sound value, the Egyptians mixing these values together to form word-shapes. These shapes instantly gave their meaning to Egyptian readers without it being necessary for them to break words down into their component parts. People who nowadays learn hieroglyphs pick up this facility quickly. (They also quickly get used to the fact that Egyptians normally wrote from right to left – as reflected in the spelling of words in this book – although in certain decorative contexts a left-to-right order was followed and the hieroglyphs themselves were reversed.)

For example, the main sign ⊗ in 𓈖 *niwt* (*niwet*), which means 'city', both conveys its sound value and acts as a determinative (see no. 32). The single stroke ı is added to emphasize that its core meaning is being referred to – that it is an ideograph – and so could also be said to be acting as a determinative (for the category 'signs as ideographs'), while the sign ◠, a picture of a small cake that writes the single letter *t*, indicates that it belongs to the feminine category. Apart from a similarly sounding word for 'underworld' used in specialized mythological texts, the main sign ⊗ is not used to write any other word. It is, however, normally added to the names of towns and cities as a determinative, to show to what general category of phenomena, namely towns, the names belong.

'City', where the dominant sign is a simplified plan of crossing streets, is an easily recognizable symbol of a city or town. The verb 'to love', 𓌻 *mri* (*meri*), by contrast, uses a sign depicting an agricultural hoe in no way related to the concept of love. Although it has not yet been identified in texts, there must have been a word for hoe that had two dominant consonants, *m* + *r*. A convention developed that other words in which *m* + *r* were prominent, including the verb 'to love', should be written with the hoe hieroglyph. From familiarity, on seeing the sign for hoe in a certain context – for example, in temples where the king was 'beloved' of the local god – an Egyptian would immediately read the word 'love'.

Ancient Egyptian was a living oral language and most hieroglyphs represent the sounds of consonants and certain emphatically expressed vowels. More weakly spoken vowels, which changed with different grammatical usage, were left unwritten, as in modern standard Arabic. Because Egyptian words were not fully written out and the language is dead we cannot speak it as an ancient Egyptian would have done. Too many nuances of pronunciation are lost. We know approximately what sound each of the hieroglyphs stands for and this gives us a rough framework that we can transfer to our own alphabet, a process called transliteration. It is a convention to render transliterations in italic. Many of the consonant sounds are the same as in English, but Egyptian contained a few sounds that require special alphabetic letters. It used four degrees of vocal strength in letting out the 'h' sound, distinguished in transliteration by *h*, *ḥ*, *ḫ* and *ẖ*. There are two 'a' sounds, rendered as *ꜣ* and *ꜥ*, the former more or less the English *a*, the latter with a glottal sound often heard in Arabic, and two versions of 'k', *k* and *ḳ*, again a glottal-like version. The transliteration signs *ỉ* and *w* stand for a firm 'i' or 'y' and a positive 'w'; *š*, *ḏ* and *ṯ* represent approximately the sounds 'sh', 'dj' and 'th'. The absence of most vowels means that we have to get used to seeing a word like ⌐⌐ (*pr*), which means 'house', and saying to ourselves '*per*'. Each transliteration in this book is followed by a simple English rendering, in brackets.

Buried within the hieroglyphic system is an alphabet. This has been put to good use by tourist jewellery shops in modern Egypt which offer to 'write your name in hieroglyphs' (and then cast it beautifully in a silver or gold pendant). This may be fun, but no ancient Egyptian would have used hieroglyphs in this way. When writing foreign names, Egyptians broke them down into syllables and used a set of hieroglyphs modified for this particular purpose. They did not spell names alphabetically as we do. It is tempting to assume that an alphabet is an easier system to learn and to use than hieroglyphs, but this is not necessarily true. A Western alphabet, although consisting of far fewer signs, is an arbitrary set of symbols not anchored in a representation of the world around us. The great advantage, however, of an alphabetic script is that it can be used to write any language and is not grounded in one specific culture, whereas Egyptian hieroglyphs are so intimately bound up with the ancient Egyptian language that they cannot as a full system be used to write any other language.

Hieroglyphic writing is in itself an introduction to how Egyptians thought. It is not the product of a brief period when people sat down and drew up a large table, in which signs and their phonetic values and pictorial meanings were arranged logically, with attempts to avoid duplication and to fill gaps. Instead the system looks like an accumulation of habits based around a few principles, enriched by idiosyncratic personal selection and subject to the processes of extinction and divergent growth that complex systems display over long periods of time. It is full of inconsistencies and usages that surprise us. But, despite this, it worked beautifully. When scribes sought to improve it, they simply added new variants.

The evidence for the earliest stages of hieroglyphic writing is incomplete. At least as far back as 4000 BC people making pottery scratched individual symbols onto the surface of jars, probably to mark ownership. There is a general reluctance to see this as writing, any more than watching traffic lights change or interpreting facial expressions can be said to constitute reading, even though information is being transmitted. In 1988, many small bone and ivory tags inscribed with groups of signs, usually one or two simple pictures followed by a numeral, were discovered in a tomb at Abydos dating to around 3150 BC, a century and a half before the 1st Dynasty. These are the earliest examples of writing so far found in Egypt; the signs, even though few in number, seem to follow rules and can be linked to hieroglyphic signs of later periods. From the beginning of the 1st Dynasty short texts appear, using quite an extensive set of signs, which no one doubts are examples of proper hieroglyphic writing. The texts are brief and record the names of kings, important events and elements of the administrative system. They have proved insufficient, however, for charting the detailed development of the writing system, hieroglyph by hieroglyph. We have to wait another five or six centuries, until the latter part of the Old Kingdom, to encounter narrative texts (carved in stone) of any significant length and examples of texts written on papyrus – by this time the system had reached a mature stage. All of the translations of texts used in this book date to no earlier than this period.

Many of the written sources – stories, useful advice on how to live contained within manuals of instruction written by famous sages, love poems, private letters – communicate with us fairly directly. Other sources are philosophical speculations about the nature of existence, written by priests. They created in intricate detail an 'Otherworld' in which the forces that governed existence – especially the sun god – struggled to keep the universe in equilibrium. The 'Book of the Dead', a collection of utterances or spells, was one popular religious text that equipped the spirit of its dead owner with knowledge to navigate safely through this complicated and dangerous realm.

The sources that depict the Otherworld took much knowledge for granted, and did not lay out a system of religious thought. The Egyptians, familiar with the details, found no need for simple explanation of this complex world. They felt enriched by alternative explanations laid side by side, accepting an ambiguity and incompleteness of knowledge. Although they argued legal cases in courts of law, they did not apply an adversarial style – which aims for a single correct verdict – to speculative knowledge. So the gods simultaneously displayed human fallibilities subject to weaknesses of body and conduct, while representing philosophical ideals, such as justice, truth, evil and power, and the fundamental elements of the universe. Reading Egyptian religious texts can be a bewildering experience as we try to enter a distinct cultural mindset.

The single ideographic hieroglyphic signs provide us with one way of exploring the unique Egyptian world. They do not paint a complete picture, however, for not all significant areas of experience were covered by their own distinctive hieroglyph, and many important words and concepts used a dominant sign which was based on phonetic similarity rather than direct representation, as explained earlier with the verb 'to love'. Nonetheless, a choice of 100 hieroglyphs presents an initial sketch of the ancient Egyptian world from specifically Egyptian concepts and knowledge. If we want to think like an Egyptian we need to think hieroglyphs.

Here, I have created an album of snapshots of what it was like to be an ancient Egyptian. Part of that experience is recreated in the order in which I have presented the hieroglyphs. Modern conventions encourage us to index a broad field of knowledge in alphabetic order, even though this is conceptually arbitrary. The Egyptians did not attach the same degree of importance to the initial letters of words. One long text, written around 1000 BC by the ancient scholar Amenemope, sets out a scheme of knowledge in the form of a word list. He provides no explanations for the individual words, but they are arranged according to a progression of association. Sometimes association runs smoothly, but sometimes large jumps occur. His list begins with words for sky, water and earth, moves through categories of people, towns of Egypt, and types of buildings and agricultural land, and finishes up with a list of an ox's body parts. I have not emulated his order, not least because I have included categories of experience (such as 'to come into existence') whereas Amenemope confined himself to concrete nouns. But I have tried to follow a flow of associations, beginning with the visible world around the Egyptians, just as Amenemope did.

Ancient Egyptian civilization ran its course in roughly 3000 years, from around 3000 BC until a time within the life of the Roman Empire. The familiar images of ancient Egypt – pyramids, Tutankhamun, animal mummies and temples such as Edfu that have survived almost complete – belong to different periods within this span and are not necessarily typical outside these periods. I have largely ignored time distinctions, though, and have drawn examples from the full breadth of Egyptian civilization, to develop a picture of ancient Egypt that is different from that of any other society.

My main concession to the long time-span covered is to tie some examples to the scheme of Egyptian dynasties. Ancient Egypt was ruled by hereditary kings (Pharaohs) from a succession of royal families, or dynasties. The dynasties were set in order and numbered from one to 30, not long after the last dynasty had departed, by an Egyptian priest named Manetho. He lived under one of the Greek-speaking kings who succeeded Alexander the Great (who had conquered Egypt in 332 BC). Two thousand years later, Manetho's scheme remains useful in a rough-and-ready way. Modern historians group the dynasties into broader periods: the Old Kingdom, the Middle Kingdom, the New Kingdom and the Late Period, separated by three Intermediate Periods of divided rule and sporadic internal warfare.

I invite you to share my fascination with a society that existed before anything remotely modern intruded. Ancient Egypt shows how far a civilization can go not only without complex technology, but also without many of the ideas and systems of belief that we are inclined to accept as the bedrock of modern civilization. We understand the beginnings of the universe in a way that was unimaginable to the Egyptians, but the question 'Why?' remains unanswered, and turns many to religion just as it did the Egyptians. Personally, I feel good about modern dentistry, ambiguous about government interference in everyday life, horrified by the magnification of the scale of hatred and killing that has happened in the my lifetime and that of my parents. The ancient Egyptians wondered why the world was such a chaotic, unharmonious place. I wonder the same and am just as bewildered as they were. Ancient Egypt provides us with a measure of how far, and how little, the world has progressed in the last few thousand years.

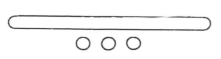

1. LAND

The heart of Egypt was and still is the floodplain of the river Nile, a narrow ribbon of green stretched across a continent wide desert. No more than 20 kilometres across in the valley proper, it reaches its greatest breadth of 200 kilometres as it fans out into a delta to join the Mediterranean coast in the north. Although the floodplain possesses subtle gradients left by slow meandering swings of the river from side to side, the valley floor gives an over-all impression of a flat land, of dark and rather heavy soil. For the word 'earth' or 'land', ⸗ *tꜣ* (*ta*), the Egyptians chose a flat, narrow sign. Beneath it, three small circles were often added, the sign for granules; land was the grainy soil beneath their feet, a physical reality, not a political entity (see no. 3, 'Grain of sand').

The borders of modern Egypt run to the Red Sea to the east; to the west and south they make a right angle and cut into the desert. The ancient Egyptian world was far smaller – no more than the muddy floor of the valley north of Aswan. The huge tracts of desert did not belong. A common name that the ancient Egyptians used for their homeland, in reference to its soil colour, was *Kmt* (*Kemet*), 'the black land'. In stepping from the valley to the desert, from the 'black' to the 'red', the ancient Egyptians were already leaving their country. In their mythology, the ram-headed creator-god Khnum fashioned human beings from clay on a potter's wheel; Egyptians associated themselves with the mud of their soil, not the sand of the desert.

Even allowing for wide margins of error in our calculations, at the time the pyramids were built the inhabitants of the whole of Egypt would have fitted into one of the larger suburbs of modern Cairo. Compared to today, the people and their dwellings would have been far less obtrusive. The basis of their lives was tilling the rich soil, and the whole population, from the peasant in his tiny house to the king in his sprawling painted palace, lived in buildings whose walls, floors and ceilings were made from mud. We know from their writings that the ancient Egyptians intended to be remembered through buildings of stone which would endure 'for millions of years'; but these were tombs and temples, not places for the living.

The valley and the delta were treated as separate 'lands' in their own right. The Egyptians constructed a myth that, at a time in the distant past, each 'land' had been a discrete kingdom, with its own symbols, including a distinctive crown. Each had its own name, and the modern convention is to translate these as Upper and Lower Egypt, for the south and the north, respectively. The kingdom of Egypt was always 'the two lands' ⚏, or more simply ⚌ *t3wy* (*tawy*), and each king was 'lord of the two lands' ⚎ *nb t3wy* (*neb tawy*). The coronation of a new king was a ceremony symbolically re-unifying the two lands. A design of two plants knotted together, found on the walls of temples and palaces, represented the binding of the two kingdoms. Over the kings reigned the supreme god, Amun-Ra, 'lord of the thrones of the two lands'.

Today the delta, the north, is the more prosperous part of Egypt, and those who live there and who are naturally more exposed to the cultures of the Mediterranean and of the lands to the north-east tend to see the people who live south of Cairo as rough and provincial. It may not always have been so. For the first half of its ancient history, between approximately 3000 and 1300 BC, the ruling families of kings came from the south. Their main city, Thebes, served as the ceremonial centre for the whole country. During the third main historical era (the New Kingdom) it was here that kings were buried (in the Valley of Kings), even when, during the later years, they were men from the north. Thebes was not, though, the equivalent of a modern capital. The main royal residence, Memphis, where government was centred, remained in the north, closer to the delta. One ancient source described it as '"the balance of the two lands" in which Upper and Lower Egypt had been weighed'.

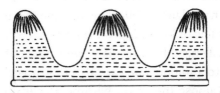

2. DESERT

The desert for most Egyptians was a crust of coarse sand and pebbles over horizontal layers of limestone or sandstone. Only those who ventured far to the west – to the area of the Kharga oasis – would have seen the desert of our popular imagination, a sea of sand dunes. Over huge areas, especially to the east of the Nile, the flow from torrential rains has cut the desert surface into networks of valleys, often with precipitous sides: they are nowadays named after the word 'wadi', originally an Arabic term, meaning a valley, that is dry except in the rainy season. Further still to the east much harder rocks rise up into jagged hills and low mountains that extend to the Red Sea.

The hieroglyph for desert depicts a broken landscape, with three rounded hills separated by deep valleys. It was added as a determinative sign to words for distant places beyond the Egyptian borders, such as 'east' and 'west', and for 'valley' and 'cemetery' – cemeteries often lay on the desert margin (see no. 36, 'Cemetery').

The word ⌒ ḫȝst (*khaset*) denoted desert, hill country and foreign land, all at once. In time it took on an ominous quality, especially when applied to the lands to the north-east. These were home to rulers whose ambitions matched those of Egyptian kings and who, from time to time, saw Egypt as an enticing target for their own conquests. In the 17th century BC, the 'rulers of foreign lands', from a homeland in Palestine, became the 'foreign rulers' of Egypt. This line of kings, called the Hyksos, ruled for two centuries until challenged by a revolt started at Thebes, which had been reduced to a minor-state capital with its own line of kings. Under King Kamose the revolt became a civil war, eventually resulting in the expulsion of the hated 'Asiatics', as the foreign rulers and their people were also called. This event marked the beginning of the New Kingdom.

In another Egyptian defeat around 525 BC, towards the end of Egyptian civilization, the Persian King Cambyses took control of the country. He was described as 'the great prince of all the foreign lands' by one of his leading Egyptian collaborators, a priest named Udjahor-resenet, who realized that only by transferring his loyalty would his temple and its traditional cults survive and prosper. Udjahor-resenet served for a time, perhaps as a physician, in the Persian court in the land of Elam (probably in the city of Susa), in the part of the Mesopotamian plain that lies in modern Iran. His plan succeeded. He returned to Egypt with a commission to re-endow the centre of learning (which the Egyptians called the 'House of Life', see no. 82, 'Scribal kit'), attached to his beloved temple.

The mindset of Egyptians was strongly influenced by the hostile, mountainous, foreign lands that surrounded them. It was a duty of kings to conquer threatening enemies, who were named in lists on the outside walls of temples. To the title of each enemy land was added the 'desert' hieroglyph, even if they were not desert places. These included places in Syria, Babylonia (which was flat and fertile and too far from Egypt to be conquered) and Crete (which was mountainous and was also never conquered by Egypt). In their claims to conquest the lists contained an element of wishful thinking.

3. GRAIN (OF SAND)

The hieroglyph for 'land' is often accompanied by the sign for a grain, a tiny circle. This is either repeated three times ∘∘∘ or shown once with three small vertical strokes added ı ı ı , to indicate that there are normally many. Signs of this kind, examples of determinatives, are added to the basically phonetic hieroglyphs that spelled nouns and verbs, in order to point to a broader family to which an individual word belongs. From signs of this kind we can learn how Egyptians grouped and classified their world, even though they appear not to have given much conscious thought to systems of classification.

'Land' is granular, as is 'sand' when found in the desert and in the riverbank (though not 'mud' which takes a different determinative, ⊐ , linking it to irrigation canals). Equally granular is 'salt', which also occurs widely in the desert, almost like a variant of sand. 'Natron', a salty lake deposit, is part of the same family. Its principal source is the Wadi Natrun, an area of dried lakebeds in the western desert. It is a natural drying agent, absorbing moisture. It was the key ingredient in the making of mummies, a process of thoroughly drying out human or animal tissue, achieved by heaping natron over the corpse (see no. 38, 'Mummy'). Natron was also an agent of purification. It was sprinkled on the ground in sacred buildings, and it was drunk in solution to cleanse priests before they entered a period of service in the temple. Charges were brought against one priest of Elephantine who entered upon his temple duties after only seven of his ten days of purification. His punishment is not recorded.

The desert produced other valued minerals and precious stones grouped in the same general category, which extended from the granular to the pebbly. 'Amethyst' and 'turquoise' are two. A third is 'eye paint', or kohl – in the historic periods this was usually finely ground grey galena (lead sulphide), probably mixed with water (or water and gum) to make a paste. The green mineral 'malachite', the principal ore of copper, and the metallic 'copper' derived from it by smelting, both use ∘∘∘ as their determinative, as do words for metals generally, for example 'gold' (see no. 87), 'silver', 'bronze' (see no. 88) and 'iron'. Here the original earthy mineral nature of the substance has been remembered despite the fact that the finished appearance of metal is hard, often shiny and definitely non-granular.

The granular sign ∘∘∘ also extends to cover plant material. Our identification of Egyptian names for plants, known primarily from medical texts, is frequently uncertain. But when plant elements use ∘∘∘ as a determinative it is likely that seeds or fruits are being referred to, such as long beans, sesame seed, lentils and chickpeas, all staples of the Egyptian diet. Another important ingredient of Egyptian life was incense, the aromatic resin from, among others, myrrh, frankincense and pistacia trees – this takes the same determinative because the Egyptians normally used it in pellet form to burn in their temples and homes. One granular group keeps its own sign, ∘∘∘. This is used as a determinative for the several varieties of grain that the Egyptians recognized, including barley, Upper Egyptian barley and emmer wheat.

A common variant for cereals is ⪑, a measuring vessel with grains pouring out. Cereal grain was the subject of an administrative system so huge that it formed a separate category in the experience of life.

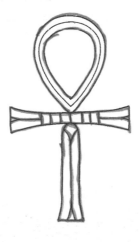

4. LIFE

In giving sand and lentils the same hieroglyphic determinative the Egyptians were acknowledging an accidental physical similarity between two quite different substances. Yet they instinctively recognized that things that pass through a cycle from birth or (in the case of plants) germination to death shared the special property of having life.

The word for 'life', ⚬ ☥ ꜥnḫ (ankh), always uses one distinctive hieroglyphic sign, a cross in which the upper vertical element is replaced by a circular shape. We do not know exactly what the object was. When internal details are added to the circular section, as is sometimes the case, the circle resembles a woven braid, and it could be a twisted shape made from plant stems around harvest time, intended to bring good fortune. The word for this object possesses a similar set of consonants to the unrelated word for 'life', and so the sign became the standard hieroglyph used in writing the latter.

Egyptian artists took advantage of this sign's shape and drew it as something that could be grasped in the hand, usually by one of the gods. In endlessly multiplied scenes carved on temple walls, gods present the sign of life to the king. Streams of life-signs cascade over him, poured from water vessels. Egypt was ruled by a line of hereditary kings who were believed to be half-divine. Scenes in two temples (of Queen Hatshepsut at Deir el-Bahari and of King Amenhetep III at Luxor) record the moment of the reigning monarch's divine birth, when the god Amun, having taken on the form of the previous king, makes his queen pregnant. With exquisite delicacy the couple sit opposite one another, hands and arms touching, and Amun raises the sign of life to the queen's face.

Death was to be feared: 'Life is given to the peaceful, death is given to the criminal.' The Egyptians understood death as a human condition, and there was no comparison made with the lifelessness or inertness of, say, minerals – with one significant exception. The work of the sculptor was to 'bring to life' the statues and images he created, and so we read of a 'living statue'. This was not just a turn of phrase. The final stage in the making of a statue (as well as the making of a mummy) was the performance of an elaborate ceremony, Opening the Mouth, in which the priest touched the mouth of the statue with an adze (a tool similar to an axe, with an arched blade at right angles to the handle) and so symbolically opened it (see no. 96, 'Statue'). No statue or memorial was complete without its name (far more important than its resemblance to the owner). The person (usually a relative) who commissioned the work might add his own name as the person who had 'brought to life' the owner's name.

The life cycle of crops prompted a different line of thought. Their seeds appear just prior to the death of the plant, and after a seemingly lifeless interval in the earth, the plant grows again. Here was a metaphor for personal resurrection after death. As the deceased says in a text on a coffin, 'I am emmer [wheat] and I will not perish.' The Egyptian hope of resurrection centred on the god Osiris, always shown swathed in the wrappings of mummification, who ruled over the kingdom of the dead. In mythical time, when a ruler on earth, he had suffered death at the hand of his brother Seth, but had been brought back to life by the ministrations of his mother Isis. Through this triumph he offered the prospect of life after death to whoever identified themselves with him. The myth inspired the making of wooden frames in the shape of Osiris, filled with soil and planted with barley seeds. Their germination simulated the hoped-for resurrection of the body. Several of these frames were buried with kings, one of them Tutankhamun, in the Valley of Kings at Thebes.

The Egyptians also imagined an island or mound at the beginning of time, rising from a primaeval expanse of lifeless waters (see no. 8, 'Water'), on which life made its first appearance, in the form of vegetation. This image was adapted for the cult of Osiris and became another metaphor of resurrection (see no. 34, 'Mound').

Death was the precursor to further life. The spirit (see no. 73) lived on – people hoped after death to 'repeat life', and a 'lord of life' was a term for one's coffin or sarcophagus. This was not the life of reincarnation, however. It was an existence spent partly around the tomb and partly in the kingdom of Osiris. The dead remained invisible to the living; but the living could communicate with the dead, by writing letters and leaving these at the tomb.

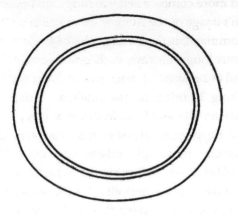

5. SUN

The Egyptians found one source of life in the power of the sun, even though its scorching heat – separately identified as the eye of the sun – was to be feared. As far back as the 5th Dynasty, King Neuserra (c. 2430 BC) had built a temple to the sun-god Ra not far from his pyramid. Its walls were decorated with detailed and brightly coloured scenes celebrating the rich and varied plant and animal life of the three seasons of the Egyptian year.

The greatest exponent of the belief that the sun gave life to the natural world, as well as to humans, was King Akhenaten, who reigned for 17 years (1352–1336 BC) at the height of Egypt's imperial period, the New Kingdom. Using the great power and wealth at his disposal he attempted to reduce the religion of his country, as he saw it, to its basic premise – what mattered most was life, and this came only from a force which emanated from the daytime sun (the Egyptian name for which was Aten), originally a manifestation of Ra, the sun-god. All else in the spiritual realm was either irrelevant or blasphemous. He failed, seemingly on account of his intolerance towards other traditional cults which offered more complex and varied spiritual experiences.

Akhenaten's image of the Aten, as carved on every temple wall built at his command, is the circular disc of the sun from which splay numerous long thin rays, each one ending in a hand elegantly profiled in a gesture of reaching out. Aten has the status of an Egyptian king. Its titles, like the king's, are written inside two cartouches (see no. 55), and from its disc emerges a cobra, one of the symbols of Egyptian royal power. It selects the royal family for unique treatment; in temple reliefs, where the rays touch Akhenaten and his queen, Nefertiti, the rays offer the hieroglyph for 'life', which they do nowhere else. Yet the universalism of the Aten's power to create was stated clearly: 'You made the earth as you wished, you alone; all peoples, herds, and flocks . . . the lands of Syria and Kush, the land of Egypt.' The Aten's power extended to the creation of the languages and skin colours of foreign peoples.

Akhenaten's simple vision of the sun temporarily replaced an older, more complex view. Egyptian religion had always held the sun as supreme power, but this idea was developed further by Egyptian priests. They imagined the sun in a splendid boat (see no. 45, 'Sacred barque'), accompanied by other divine beings who aided its journey across the sky. In pictures designed for tombs they had developed in great detail a hidden region of the night through which the sun had to pass, beset with dangers from grotesque demons (see no. 47, 'Otherworld'). Transformed into an abstract concept of power rather than something defined by direct observation, the sun's identity was merged with that of the supreme god of the city of Thebes, Amun, whose normal image was that of a man wearing a tall plumed crown. Amun became interchangeably Amun-Ra, 'king of the gods', yet still the recipient of hymns to the visible sun. It was this loss of the sun's unique character, and assumption of human identity, which prompted Akhenaten to react as he did and to turn to a simpler, truer faith.

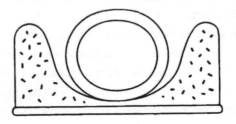

6. HORIZON

The Egyptians gave particular importance to the position and the moment of the sun's first appearance at dawn when, in an often clear sky, a sudden point of intense light rolls swiftly upwards and expands into a full incandescent orb. Despite the fact that for the people of the Nile delta the horizon was a flat expanse of green fields, marsh and trees, the image chosen to capture the essence of sunrise was a fragment of the eastern desert plateau broken by a valley. The hieroglyph marks the word 'horizon', 𓈍 ꜣḫt (*akhet*), which has both literal and metaphorical meanings.

The winged god Horus, shaped like a falcon, was associated with sunrise and solar light. He was one of the first gods depicted in hieroglyphic art (in the 1st Dynasty, c. 2900 BC), a falcon in a boat borne aloft on a pair of wings. A winged disc was often carved above temple gateways. When his name was combined with 'horizon' into 'Horus of the horizon' (Horakhty), he was the recipient of prayers, addressed directly to the visible morning sun from the top of a platform in an open-air sanctuary. To reinforce the solar aspect, the name of the sun-god Ra was often added to create the compound name Ra-Horakhty. So central was this image to the Egyptians that even Akhenaten retained it in his new fundamental faith and 'Ra-Horus of the horizon' remained an epithet of the Aten.

The hieroglyph 'horizon' also refers to the place of sunset, and more widely the rim of the sky and the abode of the gods. It gave rise to the word 'horizon dwellers', an evocative term for the inhabitants of a land to the south that was so far distant as to have no proper name (in modern terms probably central Sudan). As a striking visual image for a radiant, powerful point in the landscape, 'horizon' became a metaphor for a grand and special building, sometimes expanded to 'horizon of eternity' where the thought was perhaps that the gleaming presence of the sun would remain forever fixed. A temple, a royal palace, the tomb of the king, an important cemetery: all could be called a 'horizon (of eternity)'. The most memorable example lies in the name that King Akhenaten gave to his new city dedicated to the worship of the sun's disc, namely Akhetaten, 'the horizon of the disc' (or Aten). This is the modern archaeological site of Tell el-Amarna, which does indeed nestle in front of a horizon of high desert, cut by deep valleys, to the east. Some see in this a literal echo of the shape of the sign.

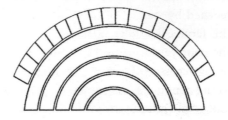

7. 'TO APPEAR'

The word 'to appear' is represented by a hieroglyph that shows the moment of sunrise – a half-visible gleaming disc. The word had a strong sense of occasion. Gods and kings 'appeared'; one of the standard titles of the king was 'lord of appearances'. During his first invasion of Palestine, in about 1460 BC, Tuthmosis III avoided his enemies (a coalition of Palestinian and Syrian city-states), took his army through a narrow defile, and overwhelmed them with a surprise attack. The decisive moment came just prior to the attack itself, with the 'appearance of the king at dawn' clad in his shining armour. Sources likened the king in his moment of 'appearance' to a warlike falcon-god Menthu. A commemorative text in the chapel built by the young Amenhetep II beside the Great Sphinx describes the king practising his martial skills in the desert near Giza: 'His majesty appeared on the chariot like Menthu in his might. He drew his bow while holding four arrows together in his fist' and aimed his arrows to pass straight through a sheet of bronze.

A king's 'appearance' was sometimes a carefully managed ceremony. Palaces, which were sometimes attached to temples, were
often built with a 'window of appearance'. A well-preserved
window pierces the side wall of the monumental outer court of
the temple of Rameses III at Medinet Habu. On the inside stood
a platform, reached by stairs, on which the king, perhaps with
members of his family, would stand. This raised him well above
the level of the courtyard outside where members of the court
gathered. Leaning across a patterned cushion laid on the window
sill the king would announce the promotion of one of his followers, or hand out costly gifts as rewards. Several examples of this
ceremony occur in scenes of court life depicted in the tombs of
Akhenaten's officials at Tell el-Amarna. Short hieroglyphic texts
quote the words of soldiers and servants as they admire the recipient's good fortune: 'For whom is this shouting being made, my
boy?' cries one. 'The shouting is being made for . . . Ay and Tiyi
(his wife): they have become people of gold,' comes the answer.
King Horemheb, an ex-general, more prosaically used his 'window
of appearance' as a means of rewarding the detachment of soldiers currently on bodyguard duty.

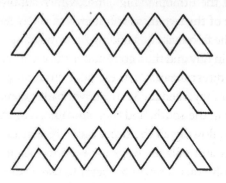

8. WATER

The richness and variety of life in the Nile valley depends upon an abundance of water, provided by the river. The depiction of water is simple enough, a stack of three zigzag lines. On their own these lines write the word 'water', and they can be added as a determinative to related words, such as 'wave', 'sweat' and 'to drink'. Zigzags placed vertically are used in another hieroglyph ▭ to represent an enclosed body of water and write the word for 'lake', or 'pool'. On a much larger scale artists used the convention of zigzag lines to decorate the outlines of ornamental pools painted, for example, on the floors of Akhenaten's palaces at Tell el-Amarna.

The flow of the Nile has now been regulated by a series of dams, but for an ancient Egyptian the most arresting image of water was the Nile in flood, the annual inundation. The immense length of the Nile meant that, even when the Egyptians occupied the northern parts of what is now Sudan, it still entered their world broad and swollen with water and greatly varying in volume from one part of the year to another. Only since the 19th century have we understood that the variation is due to the monsoon rains of the Ethiopian highlands, which supply much of the water to one of the two main tributaries of the Nile, the so-called Blue Nile. The floodwaters, building up slowly but steadily, would reach Egypt in July and then continue northwards until dispersing into the Mediterranean. At their peak in September during a 'normal' year they filled the vertical river banks as high as seven or eight metres in the south, and then spread across the fields as far as the desert, flowing all the time, a slowly swirling unstoppable force. Towns and villages were turned into islands, their occupants anxiously considering what steps to take if the flood became unusually high. Farmers worked to benefit their land by directing some of the flow to irrigation basins.

Since at least as early as the 1st Dynasty (c. 3000 BC) Egyptians measured the maximum height of the inundation each year, either by taking readings from a graduated marker or by carving each year's height into a conveniently located stone. The main reason for doing this was probably to seek reassurance, for too low or too high a flood level brought dangers of famine or destruction. Famine meant not only hunger but social disorder, as the author of a hymn to the inundation wrote. If the inundation fails, 'a year's supply of food is lost. The rich man looks concerned, everyone is seen with weapons, friend does not attend to friend.'

One set of measurements to have survived from ancient times might have induced panic. They are carved on boulders at Semna in modern Sudan, 350 kilometres south of Aswan, and record water levels of between four and nine metres above those of modern experience over a period of a century at the end of the Middle Kingdom. We can only guess at the massive destruction of property and loss of life from floods of such magnitude.

Although the Nile was a visible and unpredictable power, the Egyptians gave it a benign spiritual identity. The Nile's god was Haapy, a corpulent male figure whose obesity expressed abundance. Images show him bearing fish and water plants, and

coloured him blue or green, and zigzags of water often cover his
body. Worship of Haapy differed from the worship of other standard deities, who were usually rooted in one place. His annual
feast was at the time of the inundation, but as the wording of the
hymn of praise sung to him acknowledges: 'No one knows the
place he's in; his cavern is not found in books. He has no shrines,
no portions [offerings], no service of his choice.'

In Akhenaten's hymn to the Aten, the inundation becomes an
instrument of the sun-god's power: 'You make the inundation
from the underworld. You bring it to [the place] you wish in order
to cause the subjects to live.' Similarly the Aten is praised for the
falling of rain which, as part of a more generous view of the
world outside Egypt's border, benefits foreign lands: 'You have
granted an inundation in heaven, that it might descend for them
(the people of distant lands) and make torrents upon the mountains, like the great sea, to soak their fields.'

From classical Greece to the Renaissance the widespread view in
Europe and the Middle East was that all matter was a mixture of
four primary substances: fire, air, water and earth. This was the
basis of alchemy. The Egyptians displayed little or no interest in
thinking of physical matter in this way. Water was taken for
granted. Yet water did have a profound, spiritual role. In Egyptian
theology, Nun was the name given to the 'primaeval waters' or
'chaos'. It was the source of existence, and from it emerged the sun-
god Ra and other divine beings, including Shu, the god of light. Nun
became a metaphor for waters in the cavernous 'underworld' origin
of the Nile. The Nile's inundation was a manifestation of Nun, as
was the underground water that filled up domestic wells. The
Egyptians took pleasure in creating artificial pools containing fish,
fowl and lotus plants, and imagined them existing in the afterlife. In
an artificial lake measuring two by one kilometres dug in the reign
of Amenhetep III as a place for the celebration of his jubilee festival
(see no. 95, 'Festival'), it was said that, 'Nun is happy in its lake at
every season.'

Nun was made up of four primary properties of non-existence

described by words which are hard to translate meaningfully, but we guess at terms such as 'infinity, nothingness, nowhere and darkness' or 'endlessness, watery chaos, darkness and hiddenness'. Each of these properties had a male and female counterpart, creating a set of eight properties believed to be the basis of all existence. Today we can do little more than recognize the ancient Egyptians' attempt at a profound understanding of where energy and visible forms come from, couched as they were in a style of expression that has left no residual tradition we can latch on to. Behind the rather concrete descriptions and visualizations of existence that so mark ancient Egyptian culture, and which often come across to us as somewhat naïve, were minds that wrestled with complex philosophical questions.

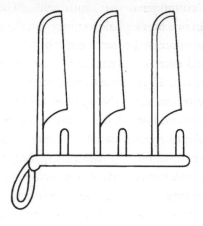

9. FIELD / COUNTRYSIDE

Saturated once a year by the flooding of the Nile, the soil of the flat land supported rich plant life, both wild and cultivated. The sign used in writing the word for field or country – 𓇏 *sḫt* (*sekhet*), in contrast to the word 𓊖, 'town' or 'city' – shows stylized reeds growing from the flat soil base. In modern Egypt the pressure of a rapidly growing population and an international, competitive economy have made land an expensive commodity, and wherever reclamation is feasible it is undertaken, currently on schemes that reach far into the desert. It was different in ancient times. Land was relatively cheap, and agricultural abundance seems to have come easily. We will never know for sure, but it is very likely that farmed land did not cover anywhere near the whole floor of the valley and delta. Consequently the 'countryside' was a mixture of farmland and places where natural vegetation grew tall and lush, usually in waterlogged or swampy ground. Here the goddess of the marsh (Sekhet, who took her name from the word for countryside, *sḫt*) could be encountered. A man who spent his days working in the countryside, as peasant or fisherman or fowler, was a 'countryman' or 'landsman', 𓋴𓈅𓏥 *sḫty* (*sekhty*), characterized in one literary tale as innocent, eloquent and representative of the oppressed common man.

The educated elite had a romantic view of the countryside. Part of the charm of Egyptian art arises from the scenes of peaceful country life recorded on the walls of tomb chapels. Peasants plough the fields and harvest the crops, while above them short lines of hieroglyphs record snatches of their calls to each other. Women gleaners squabble. In towering papyrus thickets the lordly owner of the tomb hunts birds and spears fish, accompanied by his family. In reality, as archaeological excavation reveals, most Egyptians lived in small and huddled mud-brick towns, and men of any standing must have spent part of their lives in offices. The art of tomb walls represents the escape to the countryside that the affluent scribal class yearned for, and that a few accomplished through owning country estates and villas. Presumably the peasants who did all the work saw things differently, but they have left no voice of their own.

10. PAPYRUS COLUMN

Wilderness wetlands barely survive now in Egypt but in the past they were a distinctive feature of the landscape, although not large enough to support a human population with a special way of life, such as the Marsh Arabs of southern Iraq. The dominant plant species was the papyrus (*Cyperus papyrus*) which had become almost extinct in Egypt by the 20th century AD (though it has been reintroduced to serve tourism). It grew greater than human height, it had a tough fibrous stem with a triangular section, and it supported a flowering head of numerous filaments. The stem when thinly sliced provided the raw material for an early equivalent of paper, 'papyrus' (see no. 84).

For some of the vast tracts of papyrus marshlands the Egyptians used words which took a special determinative, a picture of a papyrus clump, 𓇗. These marshes were found mostly in the delta, to such an extent that the papyrus plant served as the symbol for this part of Egypt. The teeming wildlife and the

impenetrability of the tall dense vegetation gave a sense of spiritual presence to the delta marshes. Egyptians imagined a
mythical haven, Chemnis, to exist there, supposedly located near
the city of Buto in the north-western delta. The myth concerned
the murderous quarrel within the family of the god Osiris,
between his son Horus and his rival Seth, over the inheritance of
the kingship of Egypt. On Chemnis the infant Horus was suckled
and protected from Seth by a goddess – who was sometimes
named Isis and sometimes Hathor – in the form of a cow. The
Greek traveller Herodotus, writing in the 5th century BC, says
that he saw Chemnis in a lake beside the temple at Buto. He was
told that it was a 'floating island', but adds sceptically, 'I never saw
it move, and it did not actually look as if it were floating', perhaps
because it bore a large temple and numerous date-palms and
other trees.

The Egyptians believed that the roots of their culture were to be
found within the marshlands. The Egyptian architectural style
might be said to reflect materials of marshland origins, although
whether this is historically true or not is now hard for us to tell.
Some carved pictures from the early dynasties show houses,
shrines and perhaps palaces built from reeds, even though excavations show that the common building material by this time was
mud-brick. Later, Egyptians used stone building materials, but
would carve designs in the stone to resemble the reed buildings of
their mythical home in the marshlands. The whole papyrus plant,
either in bud or with its flowering spray stylized into a bell-like pro-
file, provided the design for an architectural column in which the
shaft retained the three slightly convex faces of the natural stem.

The defining moment in the history of Egyptian architecture
came with the creation of Egypt's first monumental building in
stone, the stepped pyramid of King Djoser of the 3rd Dynasty
(c. 2660 BC), which was surrounded by a complex of shrines and
palaces. The surfaces of many of the buildings were carved to represent walls made of reeds, their corners protected by projecting
rounded bundles, and their roofs supported (unrealistically) by a
single reed stem. The designs had bold yet graceful outlines and

harmonious proportions. In later centuries the Egyptians, although never saying so explicitly, identified the architect as Imhetep, a leading figure at Djoser's court. He was eventually deified as a god of wisdom and healing.

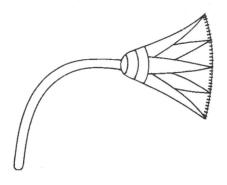

11. LOTUS

The Egyptians were attracted to paired concepts and designs expressing harmony through balanced equivalents. Around the geographical division of Upper and Lower Egypt they developed a range of paired symbols; in one the papyrus (standing for Lower Egypt) was matched either with a different kind of tall reedy plant or with the lotus (standing for Upper Egypt). Whether this reflected the natural distribution of these plants we have no way of knowing, for both papyrus and lotus long ago ceased to exist as common elements of Egypt's natural flora.

Beyond the rather artificial association with Upper Egypt, the lotus had a religious significance as a symbol of rebirth. Of the two plant varieties, the blue lotus (*Nymphaea cerulea*, as distinct from the white lotus, *Nymphaea albicans*) opens its flowers shortly after dawn and closes them later in the morning. This natural cycle was seen as a symbol of sunrise and of rebirth after death, two processes of transformation that the Egyptians were constantly and irresistibly drawn to. In a text found in Old Kingdom pyramids the deceased king is said to shine 'as the lotus at the nostril of Ra, when he appears daily on the horizon', while a later text in the Book of the Dead contains a spell for 'transforming oneself into a lotus' in the afterlife.

The blue lotus, which botanists will tell you is actually a member of the lily family, has a strong and attractive smell, and was cultivated in ponds and picked for the pleasure its fragrance gave. Inhaling the scent of a lotus flower became a common image of sensual pleasure, and was associated with alcoholic intoxication. A man tired of life converses with his soul by means of a poem: 'Death is before me today like the fragrance of lotus, like sitting on the shore of drunkenness.' We know from scientific investigation that the blossoms and roots of the blue lotus contain narcotic substances which are soluble in alcohol. It has become an attractive modern idea – although it remains hard to prove – that the Egyptians knew and exploited this property by adding the squeezed juice from the flowers to bowls of wine.

12. TREE

The date-palm tree, a cliché of Egypt today, has almost become a modern hieroglyph. Surprisingly the ancient Egyptian word for a palm tree with its own determinative, 🌴, is rare in Egyptian texts. The species which seems to have represented 'treeness' above all others was the sycamore fig (*Ficus sycomorus*), in Egyptian, 🜚 *nht* (*nehet*); it is not to be confused with the European sycamore, which is a different species. Its erect trunk and massive lateral branches gave the hieroglyph its distinctive shape, and created a natural sacred space, shady and cool. We know from tomb paintings that sitting in its shade was considered one of the delights of life after death. It was home to a goddess, whose name was either simply that of the tree itself (Nehet) or Hathor. She was a kindly goddess often approachable in places of natural spiritual presence. One of her titles was 'mistress of the sycomore', and she was especially symbolic of one particular tree, 'the southern sycomore', which grew at Memphis. Rameses II, as

part of his huge building programme, had a small temple dedicated to 'Hathor, mistress of the southern sycomore' constructed
there. The name of a famous literary hero from ancient Egypt,
Sinuhe, is literally *Sa-nehet*, 'son of the sycomore goddess'.

Although tree plantations or natural woodlands are not
referred to in ancient Egyptian texts, and are not represented by
their own hieroglyph, trees nonetheless grew widely. An Old
Kingdom official called Weni, for example, built a transport barge,
60 cubits long and 30 wide (approximately 30 × 15 metres), completed in 17 days from acacia wood at a location beside the desert
in Upper Egypt. Presumably the wood came from natural stands
of acacia close to the Nile. From boats to statues and shrines, to
common roofing poles and material for fires, wood had abundant
uses and does not seem to have been in short supply, nor was
local wood expensive to buy. A few surviving records price a log
of sycomore wood at around the same cost as a pair of woven
sandals.

The ancient Egyptian choice of quality wood was the stately
cedar (*Cedrus libani*) which grew more widely than it does now in
Syria and Lebanon. The word for cedar had its own sign, a log
stripped of its branches, ✑ . Cedar was needed for temple flagpoles and the masts of boats, and the trunks of the living cedar
tree (like those of pine and fir) exuded a resin that was thought
essential to the process of mummification, perhaps because of
its strong perfume.

To secure the supply of wood the Egyptians supported a flour-
ishing seaport, Byblos, on the Lebanese coast. Following the loss
of their empire in Palestine and Syria, at the very end of the New
Kingdom, a story was written about an employee of the temple of
Amun-Ra at Thebes, named Wenamun, who set out on a long
journey of misadventures from Thebes to Byblos to buy new
timber for the great river barge of Amun-Ra. The climax is a con-
versation between him and the prince of Byblos, who provides a
remarkable summary of Egypt's changed position in the world.
Having once been the source of craftsmanship and learning,
Egypt, he says, must now take its place as a lesser country and pay

for the resources it needs like anyone else. Wenamun, humiliatingly without money or official papers, has to send home for replacements, but as the timbers lie on the beach a pirate fleet enters the harbour and he has to flee. The end of the story has not survived.

13. PROVINCE

As Egyptian culture flourished, the people brought the alluvial land under their control by subdividing and naming the landscape. As far as we can tell, all the cultivable land of Egypt was subject to legal ownership. Indeed, transfers of ownership and resulting disputes represented a major part of ancient Egyptian legal practice. One such case ran for a whole century, ending late in the reign of Rameses II (c. 1220 BC), in the course of which official land records had been falsified. The victor, a temple treasury-scribe called Mes, was so pleased with the outcome that he had the entire history of the dispute carved on the stone walls of his tomb at Sakkara.

One basic unit of land was the ⌷ *spȝt* (*sepat*), a small province or district, which is normally translated using a Greek term, 'nome'. Upper Egypt was divided into 22 nomes, running in a continuous sequence along the Nile valley northwards from Elephantine, and varying between 10 and 65 kilometres in length. Lower Egypt had 20 nomes (beginning with the nome of

Memphis), spread across the delta in a patchwork probably shaped, in part, by the winding natural watercourses. Each nome had its own name and symbol. The sign for the 15th nome of Upper Egypt was the hare, 🐇, for example. Egyptians included basic facts of provincial geography in the decoration of temples, listing the nomes, their leading deities, and the length of the river in each. The eighth nome of Upper Egypt, for example, is given a river length which, in modern measurements, amounts to 10.5 kilometres. This information helps us reconstruct the ancient geography of Egypt.

The Egyptians grew their main crops (wheat, barley and flax for linen) in fields of sometimes irregular shape. (An ancient manual explains how to measure the areas of fields, which could be rectangular, circular, triangular or trapezoidal in shape. The given examples measure between 0.8 and 2.5 hectares). When they grew lesser crops (vegetables and spices), however, Egyptians worked the land differently. We know from ancient pictures and from actual examples found by archaeologists that they laid out flat beds consisting of grids of square plots separated by carefully made ridges of mud. The sides of each plot measured about 53 centimetres, the length of an Egyptian cubit. They then filled each plot with prepared soil in which the crops would be grown. When they counted up the plots the area of soil under cultivation was immediately given. Whether the grid that is the basis of the ▦ hieroglyph represents these gridded beds or is a simplification of the division of the land into more irregular fields, is hard to judge.

The ancient nomes, far smaller than Egypt's modern provinces, were home to families of wealth and local authority, who delighted in ostentatious displays which sometimes seemed to be a direct challenge to the king. In his tomb at Deir el-Bersheh, the governor Djehutyhetep recorded a moment when a host of his men dragged a huge alabaster statue of himself, 6.8 metres tall, from the quarry to a crossing place on the Nile and onwards to what seems to have been his palace in the city of Hermopolis. His neighbours downstream, their tombs at Beni

Hasan, maintained their own private army and were also made responsible, by the king, for a huge tract of the eastern desert. Further south, at Qau, the family of local governors built huge tombs with halls cut into the rock, terraced temples in front, and long processional causeways down to the edge of the fields. Nonetheless they had to balance their own self-interest against loyalty to their king, and included in their tombs long texts expressing their fidelity.

When royal power grew weak local governors were the ones who stood to gain most, and sometimes they even seized by force the nomes and cities of their neighbours. Ankhtyfy, a governor to the south of Thebes during a time of civil war (c. 2150 BC, early in the 1st Intermediate Period), seized the nome of his neighbour at Edfu, but then faced attacks from Thebes, his own northern neighbour, whose ruling family went on to take over the whole country and become the next line of kings.

When during the four centuries of the Late Period (8th–4th centuries BC) the country had to accept long periods of foreign rule, it was the local governors who acted as a bridge, choosing to serve the alien rulers and so maintain order and prosperity in their area. In his annals of conquest the Assyrian King Assurbanipal lists the names of 20 of them, the last being a man well known from his statues and from his huge tomb at Luxor, Menthuemhat, the mayor of Thebes. Menthuemhat lived on through further changes of rule, and became a major organizer of temple repairs. The priest of Sais, Udjahor-resenet, who worked closely with the Persian conquerors to secure benefits to his own temple in the 6th century BC, is another example.

How should we judge such men? Behaviour of this kind attracts liberal criticism in the modern world: we might expect true patriots to fight the foreign occupier. Some Egyptians, especially those who lived in the south of the country, did draw the line between themselves and foreigners, and rose in revolt on several occasions in the last centuries of Egyptian civilization. By this time, however, the resident population of Egypt included a large element of 'foreigners' who probably had limited regard for

traditional Egyptian culture. It might have seemed more sensible
to men like Menthuemhat and Udjahor-resenet to cooperate with
their foreign masters in order to preserve what remained of the
old culture.

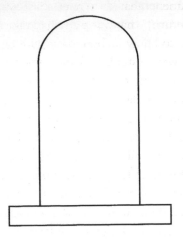

14. STELA (STANDING BLOCK OR SLAB OF STONE)

The sign depicts a round-topped slab of stone on a narrow pedestal. Egyptians loved to commemorate their lives for posterity, and stelae were used to record particular acts of piety or the history of one's life or one's outstanding personal qualities, and to list the offerings which one hoped to receive for ever more. We know the names and careers of ancient Egyptians mainly from the many thousands of stelae that have survived.

Stelae were also used to mark boundaries. Ownership of agricultural land was the basis of power and wealth in ancient Egypt. Egyptians were precise about their territory, and the boundaries of fields, cities and provinces were often permanently delineated. One of the provincial governors, Khnumhetep II of the 12th Dynasty, recorded in his tomb at Beni Hasan how the king confirmed his governorship of the area, 'having established for me a southern boundary stela and having set up a northern one like heaven, and having divided the Nile down its middle'. This was part of a wider scheme of King Amenemhat II's to re-establish 'whatever he found in disarray and [return] whatever a city had taken from its neighbour, causing city to know its boundary with city [so that] their boundary stelae were established like heaven and their river frontage known according to what was in the writings'.

The only boundary stelae to have survived in Egypt are carved into the cliffs on both sides of the Nile around King Akhenaten's new city of Tell el-Amarna. They are inscribed with a sacred oath declaring that the city will never extend beyond their limits. So important were the stelae to Akhenaten that a year after the first set was carved a second set was added, and then two years after this the king visited them, in his chariot, to repeat the oath.

It became the duty of kings to 'enlarge the boundaries of Egypt' through conquest. Around 1862 BC King Senusret III set up a boundary stela beside the river in Nubia, 350 kilometres to the south of the Egyptian frontier at Aswan, at a place called Semna. It stated: 'Any son of mine who maintains this boundary which My Majesty has made, he is a son of mine who was born to My Majesty . . . He who shall abandon it and not fight for it is indeed no son of mine.' The king set up a statue of himself at the boundary, 'that you might be inspired by it and fight on its behalf'. Three centuries later, in the New Kingdom, the southern boundary stood at more than twice the distance to the south, the result of the renewed Egyptian policy of aggression. On an isolated rock near Kurgus in what is now Sudan, King Tuthmosis I had a scene and a text carved to act as his boundary marker. Tuthmosis III subsequently added a similar one. Yet the Egyptian empire, especially in Palestine and Syria, remained fragile, and the Egyptians often found themselves fighting over territory across which many of their predecessors had already marched.

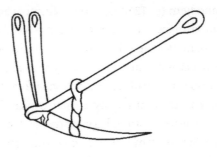

15. PLOUGH

The plough was a Near Eastern invention of the prehistoric periods and is one of the very few truly labour-saving devices that the Egyptians adopted. The wealth and success of ancient Egypt depended to a large extent on the cereal agriculture of the Nile floodplain. The fertile soil and the annual autumn flooding of the land, and its careful management by means of earthen banks and drainage ditches, gave the expectation of abundant harvests. In modern times the damming of the river has allowed farming around the year. Neither the land nor the farmer gets a natural break – whereas in ancient times farming ran through a single annual cycle which began with the inundation, followed by ploughing, planting and growing, and ending with the harvest and a lengthy period when the land rested. It is now assumed that it was at this relatively slack time that kings would send out demands for extra labour for great building projects, especially the dragging of stone for pyramids.

One Egyptian concept of the afterlife gave it an agricultural setting, the Field of Iaru, with dead members of the official class
facing an eternity of agricultural labour – something which they
would have ardently sought to avoid in life. The tomb of the
craftsman Sennedjem (c. 1250 BC), for example, shows both him
and his wife (in immaculate white garments) ploughing and har-
vesting. Sennedjem lived at a time when ideas on the relationship
between earthly existence and eternity were changing. In earlier
periods, the art on tomb walls celebrated the life of landed gentry,
set ambiguously in time, implying that this was also the life to
come. There was little room left for pictures of gods or halls of
judgement. By Sennedjem's time, however, gods had largely
crowded out the scenes of eternity as one long holiday. For the
next thousand years, until ancient Egyptian culture faded away,
tomb art avoided images of earthly pleasures, and sought instead
to safeguard the dead against unpredictable spiritual forces.
Household or personal goods were no longer buried in the tomb.
What remained were amulets and a copy of the Book of the
Dead – a set of 189 spells or chapters written on a continuous roll
of papyrus, a licence to an eternal place among the gods and
demons of the afterlife.

Even in earlier periods, however, behind the cheerful material-
ism of the tomb scenes, there lay a fear of labour conscription.
The king and the various departments of his administration had
the right to command people to carry out work such as soldiering
or building a pyramid. Egyptians feared that conscription might
reappear in the afterlife. Chapter 6 of the Book of the Dead is a
spell first encountered around 2000 BC and was in use to the end
of Egyptian civilization. It was a spell of substitution. When called
upon to do so, a manufactured figurine would stand in for the
deceased person when the summons for conscription arrived.
Who, in the next world, would issue that summons is never stated.
Even kings faced the same fate. It was evidently a visceral dread
which tells us something very important about the quality of life
in ancient Egypt. You never knew when your name would appear
on a list, even though you might be one of the elite.

The figurines, called *shabti* or *ushabti* by the Egyptians, were laid in the tomb. Chapter 6 of the Book of the Dead was often written on them, and they are shown with a hoe and a basket for carrying lumps of earth. These symbolized field labour of the most basic kind. The numbers of *ushabti*-figures multiplied during the later New Kingdom and afterwards. The ideal was a *ushabti* for every day of the year, and a complement of overseer figures (who carry a whip) to look after the *ushabti*-figures in gangs of ten, making a set of 365 *ushabti*-figures and 36 overseers – 401 in total. A papyrus receipt has survived for just such a set of 401 figures, sold for silver to a priest by the 'chief maker of amulets of the temple of Amun'. It is likely that the temple would receive a portion of the payment, if not all, illustrating that organized religion in ancient Egypt relied in large part upon conventional economic transactions.

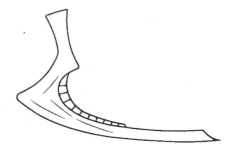

16. SICKLE

Egyptians mainly grew cereal of two kinds: emmer wheat – which does not thresh easily and has tough, spiky heads – and barley. We know from tomb scenes of the harvest, that the ears and heads of the cereal were cut quite high, leaving much of the straw standing. The cutting was done by a curved wooden sickle which sported a line of serrated flint blades on the inside edge. Flint was used for perhaps 3000 years after the introduction of copper and bronze for other kinds of cutting edges, and illustrates how, in traditional societies, individual technologies can keep going as an independent tradition if they satisfy the user.

Once gathered, the ears of emmer wheat and barley were hauled off the fields in large baskets, sometimes slung over the backs of donkeys. Their destination was a piece of hard, dry and clean ground set aside for threshing and winnowing. Here the cereals were spread out in a layer. Hoofed animals were driven back and forth across them to separate the ears from the heads.

The chaff and dust were separated by men repeatedly tossing the trodden grain into the air using a pair of wooden scoops, to allow the breeze to carry away the lighter unwanted elements. The cleaned grain was scooped into containers and heaped onto a prepared mud surface with a raised rim. Scribes, ever disdainful of manual labour, counted the scoops (which had a fixed capacity) and so measured the harvest.

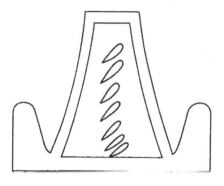

17. GRAIN PILE

Full granaries were a source of great satisfaction. It was, however, the heap of measured grain standing on a low mud platform beside the threshing floor that more readily symbolized the successful harvest and gave rise to a hieroglyph. Behind the successful harvest, and in contrast to the simplicity of the technology, lay a complex system of land management. Much of the land seems not to have been in the hands of farmers at all, but owned by temples and members of the governing class (including the royal family). They, in turn, rented out large parts of the grain lands to others, who might then employ lesser people to do the work. Even the extent to which farms existed, in the form of discrete areas of land with one owner, with a farmhouse in the middle, is far from clear. When we do have more detail, estates, especially those belonging to temples, seem to be made up of plots of land in different parts of the country, the accumulated result of centuries of buying and selling, of subdivided inheritance and of gifts and rewards.

Much depended upon the reliability of agents paid to manage the estates, whose owners would often have been busy, and distant officials. And so Egypt, like other similar ancient societies, developed systems of bureaucratic checking. Egypt was a very controlled society. No one, high or low, was ever very far from someone else's paperwork. One inevitable consequence was the deadly game played by those who cheated the system, and those paid to check and investigate. A long indictment has survived, from the reign of Rameses IV (1153–1147 BC), against a priest in the temple at Elephantine. Accusations of violence, impiety and seduction are followed by details of a major scheme, running for several years, in which boatloads of grain destined for the temple granaries were stolen. This must have involved the tacit assent of many people, and is a fine example of a 'black economy' at work. The evidence gathered was specific: someone had done a thorough investigation and was able to cite, year by year, the exact deficit of grain sacks. What the outcome was we will never know, but death for the main culprit is very likely, and perhaps mutilations for others.

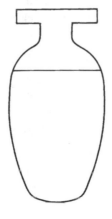

18. BEER JUG

Stored grain was wealth, and sacks of it were used as a medium of exchange, in effect as a form of money. It had, of course, a limited life in store and so could not be hoarded for too long. The constant emptying of the granaries kept wealth in circulation, never earning interest, and provided a healthy local economic stimulus. In the end, however, apart from what was set aside for next year's seed, grain was consumed, and thus it formed the principal element in the Egyptian diet. It was eaten in a wide range of baked products – breads, cakes and biscuits – and fermented into beer. Many records have survived of ration payments issued to employees, and even workers at the king's court, and they consist of so many loaves of bread and pottery jugs of beer. In one tale an unusually eloquent countryman is detained at court so that the king can secretly enjoy the countryman's well-turned speeches of complaint about injustice to the poor, and in return the king supplies him with a daily ration of

ten loaves and two jugs of beer, and sends his distant family three
sacks of grain every day.

Modern research has tried to work out how ancient Egyptian
beer was made. The process is depicted in tomb scenes, and much
can be learned through the microscopic study of beer residues
inside pottery vessels used in the brewing process. What was once
regarded as a rather crude process is now understood to have
been more sophisticated and would have allowed the brewer to
control the taste of the final product. It relied upon malting
(allowing the grains to begin to sprout and so release their sugar)
and, crucially, the mixing and blending of uncooked malt with
cooked grain or malt. What we cannot today discover, unfortu-
nately, is the taste. Most modern beers of the European tradition
have the strong bitter flavour of added hops but this plant was
unknown in ancient Egypt. Other plant flavourings might have
been added, such as coriander, but it has not yet been possible to
detect them scientifically.

Drunkenness was a yardstick of pleasure: 'If I kiss her, and her
lips are open, I am happy, even without beer' is a verse from a love
poem of the New Kingdom. Beer was enjoyed at festivals, and
days off for brewing are one cause of absenteeism in work regis-
ters of necropolis workmen of Thebes. The feasts of the goddess
Hathor seem to have been a particularly appropriate time for
drinking to excess. 'Come, walk in the place of drunkenness, that
pillared hall of diversion', invites a song to Hathor, 'Drunkards ser-
enade you by night.' One myth explains the connection.
'Mankind' (i.e. the Egyptian people) rebel against the ageing sun-
god Ra. They flee from his wrath into the desert where they are
pursued to destruction by Hathor, now no longer kindly but
an avenging goddess whose lust for blood is assuaged by red-
pigmented beer being poured over the fields as if it were an
inundation of the Nile.

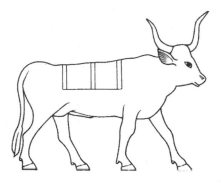

19. BULL

Perhaps on account of their size and natural dignity, the Egyptians saw cattle as, to some small degree, proximate to themselves. An Egyptian term for mankind was 'the cattle of god', and conversely the term 'herdsman of mankind' described the kindly role of the king and of the creator-god. In ancient times cattle still existed in the wild, and the fierceness of wild bulls provided a suitable image of the king, who terrifies on the battlefield. 'Victorious bull', using a more aggressively posed hieroglyphic sign, 𓄟, was a standard epithet for the king. More prosaically the same names were used for some of the body parts of humans and of cattle, such as 'ribs' and 'liver'.

Cattle were both worthy of reverence and were a practical food resource. The earliest example of a sacred animal cult is that of the Apis bull. Centred at Memphis, ancient annals as early as the 1st Dynasty (c. 3000 BC) record a 'running of the Apis bull'. There was only ever one Apis at a time, and in the later New

Kingdom and onwards until Roman times each Apis was, on death, given an expensive burial in an underground catacomb, the Serapeum.

A second cult of a sacred bull, that of Mnevis at Heliopolis across the river from Memphis, went back at least as far as the 12th Dynasty. Certain other gods drew upon animals for their appearance: the ram or ram-headed god Khnum at Elephantine is one example; the crocodile or crocodile-headed god Sebek at Kom Ombo is another. For much of Egyptian history, however, we have no knowledge that living specimens were regarded as sacred: this came during the last seven centuries or so of Egyptian civilization. Sacred animal cults then became hugely popular, and living representatives of a whole species were viewed as sacred. As a result everywhere in Egypt cemeteries appeared of mummified animals – cats, baboons, ibises, fish – sometimes in catacombs which held millions of carefully wrapped specimens.

This is not a sign, however, that the Egyptians held wildlife in special reverence. They were not vegetarians. Hunting wild animals in the desert was a sport for the king and his nobility. King Amenhetep III issued two sets of large scarabs to commemorate his hunting success, in one case against desert lions (102 kills in ten years) and in the other against wild bulls (96 in two days). It seems unlikely that the deserts adjacent to Egypt even at this time supported wildlife in these numbers and animals for the hunt may have been imported from much further to the south. Domesticated cattle was an important source of food, and prime cuts were prominent among food offerings at temples. Some temples possessed an actual slaughterhouse or slaughter-court as part of their layout. Perhaps the most striking example of acquiescence to the deaths of animals otherwise seen as god's creatures occurs at the Aten temples of King Akhenaten. Despite the pious sentiments of hymns to the sun-god, the cult of the Aten demanded the presentation of food offerings on a large scale, and so the main Aten temple was provided with a butcher's yard, and the high-priest Panehsy also held the office of 'overseer of the cattle of the Aten'.

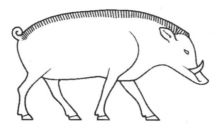

20. PIG

Certain cultures develop strong predjudices against foods that others find fully acceptable. Judaism and Islam (but not Christianity even in its Middle Eastern forms) have categorized the pig as an unclean animal not to be touched or eaten. Herodotus reported in the 5th century BC that the Egyptians considered the pig to be unclean yet maintained herds of them and sacrificed them on a particular festival. This ambiguity matches the evidence from earlier periods.

It seems that Egyptians were not prohibited from eating pig, but felt a degree of reservation. Studies of animal bones recovered during the excavation of ancient Egyptian settlements show that the pig was common. Many of the bones bear cut- and chop-marks from butchery. There are occasional pictures in tombs showing herds of pigs. An 18th Dynasty mayor of El-Kab recorded in his tomb his ownership of 1500 pigs (along with 122 cattle, 100 sheep and 1200 goats). More remarkable is a pious donation to the temple of Ptah at Memphis of 2000 pigs. Pork did not feature in religious offerings, but then neither did sheep or fish; beef and goose were what the spirits of the gods and of the dead preferred.

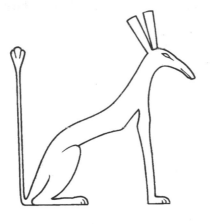

21. SETH-ANIMAL

In Egyptian mythology, Seth was the wicked rival of his brother Horus, both sons of the murdered King Osiris. Horus, the rightful claimant to the throne of Egypt, was the mythical embodiment of a loyal son, whereas Seth, who disputed Horus's claim to the throne, was simultaneously held responsible for the murder of their father. Seth's hieroglyph depicts him as an animal, a quadruped not easily identified with an actual animal species.

The god Seth was a complex figure in Egyptian thinking who defies simple definition. Occasionally the myth referred to Seth as Osiris's brother (and thus Horus's uncle): his identity varied and mutated in much the same way as his symbolic significance. He symbolized a frequently dangerous 'alternative', against which positive characteristics could be defined. One text described him as the 'oldest magician of the sacred place of the first occasion' (the time of creation).

Unlike Satan in the Christian worldview, Seth was not

portrayed as a devil beyond redemption. In the end Seth submitted to the judgement of the high court of gods, was reconciled to Horus, and settled for second place in the kingdom. In this context he became a legitimate patron god and supporter of Egyptian kingship. Two kings of the 19th Dynasty, Seti I and II, even named themselves after him, although his name still carried an ambiguous and powerful meaning. When Seti I built a temple to Osiris on a particularly lavish scale at Abydos, the artists decorating the temple chose a tactful spelling of the king's name which omitted the hieroglyph of his arch-rival Seth.

Certain qualities of Seth were also believed to be embodied within the Egyptian people; we know this from a book belonging to an ancient Egyptian scribe. Scribes – civil servants of their day – accumulated private libraries of papyri covering diverse subjects. One such library, owned by a succession of scribes from the village of craftsmen at Thebes (Deir el-Medina), included a book on how to interpret dreams. Before interpreting the dream of a client, it was necessary to place that person in a particular group, perhaps comparable to modern horoscope groupings. A surviving fragment of the papyrus lists the characteristics of a person with 'Seth' qualities: he has red hair, drinks beer and becomes aggressive, attracts women with his passion, and fights murderously with weapons. In spite of this he can be long-lived, reaching 84 years, and he is not an outsider. He can remember his dreams, and according to the details they can be interpreted as either a good or bad omen.

Seth was an essential role model who helped to explain the turmoil and divisions of the world. His hieroglyph is found attached to words for 'storm', 'tumult', 'illness' and 'nightmare'. In another pairing he represents the lands beyond the Nile valley – especially the desert – and by extension is a god of foreign places, particularly those of the Near East. In 1258 BC King Rameses II made a peace treaty with the king of Egypt's long-term enemy, the kingdom of Hatti (home of the Hittites). Both the Egyptian and the Hittite versions of the treaty have survived. Each places the treaty under the care of their gods. In the

Egyptian version, however, the Hittite gods are represented as local variants of Seth. The belief in Seth illustrates how ancient Egyptian thinking at a serious level differed from our own: whereas modern learning tends to seek logical explanations for the world around us which feed into a single grand scheme, Egyptian logic and meaning could shift depending on the immediate context.

22. RED

The hieroglyph for red depicts a flamingo, which until about a hundred years ago was still breeding in the Nile delta. To modern eyes the flamingo, which is white and pink, is a poor representative of redness, yet it made sense in the Egyptian's world. Not much else had a naturally red tone, and it has a distinctive enough outline for a hieroglyph. When Egyptians created hieroglyphic signs to write on walls of tombs and temples, they were attracted to bold clear shapes which instantly conveyed the essence of the object. If necessary (for example, no. 23, 'Sparrow'), one component part (in that case the sparrow's tail) is rotated through ninety degrees to present a more characteristic outline.

We can never know which came first, the word for red – then used to describe the flamingo – or the name of the flamingo, which then created a word for red. The separate naming of fine colour distinctions is a relatively modern phenomenon. The Egyptians managed with very few colour terms, and these covered a wide range of tonality. They had opportunities to see the colour orange, in deposits of desert sand or in the sky at sunset, but not only did they have no reason to single it out for comment, in lacking oranges they had no convenient reference colour. 'Red' could describe both the pinkness of a flamingo or the colour of blood. When paired with another hieroglyph to create the word 'red land' (another word for 'desert'), we learn that red also included what we see as oranges, greys and yellows.

In some contexts, red could stand for 'otherness', rather in the way that Seth did, which explains why Egyptians with red hair were associated with Seth. A word derived from 'red' meant 'wrath', as did the phrases 'red of heart' and 'red of face'. Red was the colour of enemies. One inexpensive way of safeguarding Egypt from attack was to write the names of hostile foreign leaders in red ink on clay figurines or pottery vessels and then bury or smash them. The gods would do the rest.

Not all red things were bad. Red ink was used to highlight significant words in texts without any negative implications, and the Red Crown was worn by the king to symbolize his rule over Lower Egypt, standing in contrast to the White Crown of Upper Egypt. Red was a common colour used to paint doors, window shutters and wooden columns in houses, presumably as a simple way to provide a contrast with the bare mud-plastered walls, which would not always have been whitewashed.

Red pigment was easy to acquire. It came as ochre from the desert, and could be made into a powder so fine it could permanently colour linen cloth, although by the 18th Dynasty the Egyptians were also dyeing cloth with madder, a red vegetable dye. In paintings, a darkish red was the preferred colour of male skin. The fact that it contrasted with the yellow skin colour for women and was used for field labourers and for officials alike is probably a sign that it stood for the positive values of maleness, since artists were themselves men.

23. SPARROW

A small brown bird, probably a sparrow, acts as the sign denoting things of ill-omen. There is nothing in written sources to suggest that small brown birds were in themselves thought to be evil or unlucky. They are in fact rarely mentioned. The sparrow hieroglyph most likely developed its meaning because it represented the least favoured of a set (in this case of birds), and it was common. In an opportunistic way this tradition became embedded in the hieroglyphic script. Words that take this determinative sign include 'small', 'empty', 'narrow', 'bad', 'to be ill', 'misery', 'injury', 'to sigh', 'ruin', 'misfortune', 'to fail', 'deprivation' and even 'evil' and 'wrongdoing'.

24. GOOD

Whereas the Egyptians had a rich vocabulary for unpleasantness they relied heavily on a single word, 'good' (*nfr*), for positive appreciation across a broad range of experience. Unlike the word for misfortune, which Egyptians associated with the sparrow, the symbol for good was not taken from the natural world by direct association. To write it they chose a sign which represented something quite unrelated (the heart and windpipe) which happened to possess the same sequence of consonants $n + f + r$. This was the standard alternative way by which hieroglyphs were selected to form part of the writing system. Once an Egyptian made the connection while learning hieroglyphs, the sign for heart and windpipe, of course, read immediately as 'good' and so would, in effect, become its symbol.

Nfr was applied to the fineness of linen, the quality of a wine (which, when particularly good, was ⚲⚲ *nfr nfr*). The king was 'the good god', one's pet name among friends was one's 'good name', and the holiday feeling was captured by the expression 'making a good day'. It also applied to provocatively attractive young women: in one story, King Sneferu, father of Khufu the builder of the Great Pyramid, takes pleasure in a boating party in which he is rowed up and down by twenty beautiful girls ('girls' is a noun derived from *nfr*) whose beauty lies in 'their limbs, their breasts and their braids' and the fact that they have not yet given birth, and who are to entertain the jaded king by wearing open bead-latticed garments instead of their normal clothes. When one of them grows petulant at having dropped a turquoise pendant overboard, a magician folds the waters back so that it can be retrieved.

The Egyptian writer Ipuwer sums up the cultural ideal of 'good' in a text of a very different tone. He begins a series of poetic statements with the phrase 'how good it is' and uses them to paint an attractive picture of Egyptian contentment; the sailing of ships on the Nile, the work of fishermen and fowlers, safe passage on the roads, the building of tombs, the creation of lakes and orchards for the gods, the drunkenness of happy people, the wearing of clean linen, the preparation of the master's bed and 'when every man's need is satisfied by a mat in the shade'.

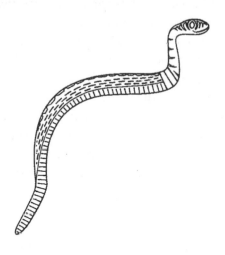

25. SERPENT

Out of a primitive aversion to snakes, which probably goes beyond the fear of being bitten, emerges an image of hostility: a long sinuous serpent. While Egyptians could relate to Seth with his human characteristics, serpents were more distant from human understanding. They had an ominous presence in the afterlife, which was simultanously the abode of the gods and of the dead (see no. 47, 'Otherworld'). Their sinuous forms contrast with the human shapes that inhabit the Otherworld and wind themselves into its ordered spaces.

Serpents were generally dangerous, hostile creatures. One named serpent, Apep (Apophis), was cast as the enemy of the sun-god Ra. The title of a papyrus text which deals with their struggle is the 'Book of Knowing How Ra Came into Being and of Overthrowing Apophis'. The conflict goes back to the beginning of time. This is true for another myth, recorded on the walls of the temple of Edfu (3rd century BC), which explained why certain places were chosen as the locations of temples: they were the places where the forces of evil in the form of serpents had been defeated by companies of divine beings.

Of the various species of snake at home in Egypt today nine are dangerous to humans. A papyrus of the 4th or 3rd century BC lists 38 different types of snake, along with a description of their distinguishing features (hue, unusual size or number of fangs or behaviour), and the effect of their bite and whether this can be treated. In Egyptian mythology the venomous power of snakes could be harnessed for good. The cobra, which can reach more than two metres in length and characteristically raises its head and extends its hood when angered, became an enduring symbol of the power of the king and of the sun-god. Cobras were also a protective power for Egyptian people, who often felt that a world of spiritual forces was closer and more familiar than the gods and goddess of the temples. The fear of ghosts of dead men and women pressed in during the night: one way to protect against them was to make four serpents of clay 'with flames in their mouths', place them at the corners of any room where people were sleeping, and recite over them a short spell of protection. Clay cobra figurines have been found during the excavation of settlements and could well be the remains of this practice.

But not all serpents were even dangerous. One story told the tale of a mariner shipwrecked on a magic island on which lived a giant and genial serpent 30 cubits long (15.5 metres), with the appearance of a living Egyptian statue: 'His beard was over two cubits long; his body was overlaid with gold, his eyebrows were of real lapis lazuli.' The serpent reveals that he is the sole survivor from a catastrophe, when fire from heaven burned up the family of 75 other serpents, 'not counting a little daughter whom I had obtained through prayer'. Out of gratitude for the temporary relief from his loneliness, he heaps rewards on the sailor at the moment when a ship comes to rescue him (and the island disappears beneath the waves).

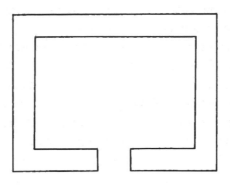

26. HOUSE

Prehistoric Egyptians lived in small circular huts. The hieroglyphic system developed, however, towards the end of the fourth millennium BC, when the main material for building was brick, made from mud and dried in the sun, and houses were rectangular in plan. The hieroglyph used to write the word 'house', ⌐┐ *pr* (*per*), conveys its essence, an oblong room with a single door. In reality few houses can have been as basic as this. From a fairly well documented history of house design in ancient Egypt we can see a tradition of grouping all rooms (and in larger houses they could amount to 20 or more) together under a single continuous roof rather than around a central courtyard. When courtyards were present they were at the side, and it would be here that the cooking was done, inside and over a small cylindrical clay oven which was constantly surrounded by deposits of fine ash. The focus of domestic life was a central room, sometimes furnished with brick benches only ten centimetres high on which people would squat, although wooden chairs and stools were also to be found (see no. 28, 'Mat'). The larger the house the more likely the roof of the central room, and perhaps those of other public rooms, was supported on painted wooden columns resting on circular stone column bases. Bedrooms had a prominent and slightly raised alcove, with space for a single bed. Lesser members of the household might not have had their own bedrooms. It is hard to know whether excavated houses possessed upper floors, since it is rare for walls to be preserved to more than about waist height. The frequent presence of a narrow staircase is no proof, since it might have led only to a flat roof which could itself have been used for storage and as a place for sleeping on hot summer nights.

A 'house' amounted to more than a building. A young shipborne fighter in the war against the Palestinian Hyksos kings, named Ahmose from El-Kab, 'founded a house' after his first period of service, which sounds like a phrase for getting married. The 'house' included its occupants, presided over by the 'lady of the house', ⌑⌣ nbt pr (nebet per), the most common title given to a married woman. We have a fairly detailed picture of a household from the letters written by one Hekanakht (c. 1980 BC), who seems to have been a minor official but also owned land of his own. Away from home he wrote in an argumentative style to his family about farm and domestic matters, and refers to a household of 12 people, each of whom received from him a strictly measured ration of grain. Five were sons, the eldest of whom managed the household in his father's absence. Most of the others were women, including Hekanakht's mother, and his new wife (most likely he was widowed) who was a source of conflict (see no. 66, 'To love'). Other records of households, urban rather than rural, show smaller numbers, in single figures, with far fewer children than one might expect, perhaps a consequence of a high infant mortality rate (see no. 78, 'Child'). Many households made themselves larger with servants or slaves. We do not know whether these servants slept in corners of the house or had places of their own.

As in other traditional cultures, cattle, which were too valuable to leave out at night, would share the collection of buildings that made up the house. In the Tale of Two Brothers (c. 1200 BC) the innocent and unmarried younger brother does all the heavy work, brings the cattle home at night, and after serving his elder brother and wife with food, goes off to sleep among the cattle in a stable that was part of the house compound. This harmonious picture is destroyed by the elder brother's wife who tries to seduce the younger brother and, when rejected by him, accuses him of attempted rape. It is the cattle who warn the younger brother of the presence of the elder brother waiting behind the door of the house to kill him.

The word 'house' also meant lineage. To its enemies in the civil war of the 1st Intermediate Period the kings of the north were 'the house of Khety', named after the founder. It desig nated institutions. 'The house of silver' was the Treasury, 'the house of life' was the place of learning where manuscripts were studied and copied (see no. 82, 'Scribal kit'), and the 'house of Amun' included the temple's extensive estates. Combining 'house' with a word for 'great' created the hieroglyphic group for 'great house', ⬚ *pr ꜥ₃* (*per-aa*), signifying the king's residence. In time the phrase became a polite way of referring to the king without naming him. Taken up by the compilers of the Old Testament the word has given us, via Hebrew, 'Pharaoh'.

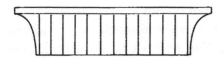

27. DOOR

The hieroglyph depicts a single door leaf with its characteristic wooden strengthening bars on the inside surface. Egyptian doors were always relatively tall and narrow, rotating on a lower wooden pivot set into a pivot block in the floor of the doorway, and kept vertical by an upper pivot held within a simple casing in the lintel. House doors were normally a single leaf, but in grander settings – the front door of a rich man's house or the main entrance to a temple – they came as pairs.

Doors allowed for privacy and helped to keep out bad weather. To look after the main door to a large property a door-keeper was hired. Although the title was lowly it was still one a man could use as a mark of status. Doors secured storerooms against theft. Instead of locks, Egyptians had only simple sliding carved wooden bolts. They sought security by winding string either between the ends of a bolt across a double-leaf door or, when the door was of a single leaf, between a bolt and a peg fixed to the door jamb. A mud sealing was then applied over the string, stamped with a distinctive design from a personal seal (see no. 83, 'Cylinder seal'). The security of storerooms could be monitored and written about in reports. Transferred to the full daily temple order of service, the unsealing and opening of the doors of the various shrines became a significant act of ritual.

At a deeper religious level doors were also seen as a means of access and closure. With their surrounding portals they marked stages on a journey through the imagined realm of the Otherworld. The dead faced a sequence of 21 doors manned by door-keepers who had to be addressed by their correct names before they would grant admission: 'Make way for me, for I know you, I know your name, and I know the name of the god who guards you.' A set of 12 similar portals, one for each hour, marked stages of the sun's perilous journey through the imagined realm of the night, painted in great detail in the tombs in the Valley of Kings at Thebes.

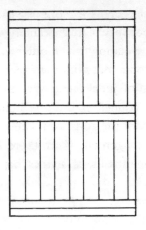

28. MAT

Modern furniture – from chairs and tables to sinks with draining-boards – tends to be high off the ground, so we rarely need to flex the lower body. We do not squat or sit flat on the floor a great deal, and often find the positions uncomfortable. For traditional societies like ancient Egypt, ground-based living was the norm. The Egyptians did make elegant wooden furniture; stools, seats, small tables and beds. Many examples are known from excavations or from ancient tomb pictures. A few were made to fold up for easy transportation. The bed of Queen Hetep-heres – mother of Khufu, builder of the Great Pyramid (c. 2589–2566 BC) – is a marvel of ingenuity and craftsmanship in the metal cladding of its pivoting joints. For any given household, however, items of wooden furniture were probably few in number and marked the status of the owner. In pictures of banquets, for example, the host and his wife sit side by side on chairs, but the guests often squat on mats on the floor, even ladies clad in the fashionable costume of the times. The hieroglyph for mat depicts a complete and almost square mat woven from plant materials. Another version of a mat is contained in the hieroglyph for 'offering place' (see no. 98).

The association between status and being seated was not consistent. There was a tradition, much older than furniture, which linked being seated on a mat with the exercise of authority, and especially the giving of judgement. We read of 'scribes of the mat' and even of a 'council of the mat', but most notably it is upon mats that many of the gods would be sitting when the dead reached the halls of judgement: 'I am there with Osiris, and my mat is his mat among the Elders,' states Chapter 124 of the Book of the Dead.

29. CAT

During the New Kingdom (1550–1070 BC) it was fashionable to include a picture of a cat in domestic scenes of husband and wife painted in tomb chapels. The cat is beneath the wife's chair, although in one tomb (of the sculptor Ipuy at Deir el-Medina) the husband also has a kitten on his lap. The cats are well observed. They gnaw bones, devour fish, spit at a goose. One is tied by a ribbon to the chair leg, another wears a bead necklace and earrings. They accompany the family on hunting parties in the marshes as if they are full members of the family. They are clearly pets; did the Egyptians give them names? The sources are silent, but this might just be because cats belonged mainly to women, and most of our sources were compiled by men. The men were happy to give names to their dogs and many examples are known. King Wahankh Intef of the 11th Dynasty even included named dogs on his tombstone.

There is one telling exception. A small limestone sarcophagus was commissioned by a crown prince of the 18th Dynasty, Thutmose. It was intended to contain a mummified cat named Tamyt, which means simply 'female cat'. The sarcophagus carries standard religious texts, and they treat Tamyt as if she had been fully human, becoming Osiris on her death, and joining the imperishable stars of heaven. It is tempting to see this as an ultimate expression of pet love; yet the completeness of Tamyt's transformation into a spiritual being might be a sign that she was actually a sacred animal.

The wild hunting instinct in cats gave them a place in the Egyptian pantheon, and this was especially so in the New Kingdom and later. Male cats, sometimes armed with a knife, appear as demons in the Otherworld, helping to kill the serpent foe of the sun god. More people worshipped a female cat, however, incorporating images connected with a fierce lioness-goddess, Sekhmet. The cult of a cat goddess was associated with the sun-god Ra, with child-bearing and with protection. The cult developed especially strongly at the city of Baset in the Nile delta, and the cat goddess was known simply as 'She of Baset' (thus, Bastet). Her festival became a major event, attracting (according to Herodotus) several hundred thousand people. Beside the city there developed a huge cemetery for cats, which had been bred, killed and carefully mummified as an expression of piety.

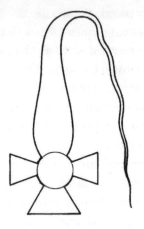

30. FIRE

When archaeologists excavate an ancient settlement in Egypt they work through layer after layer of earthy debris to expose the foundations of ancient buildings. Much of the debris is brick rubble but also common is ash from fires. In their houses and places of work fires were never far from ancient Egyptians. The quantities of ash are sometimes surprising. Part of an unusually well-preserved building at Elephantine was used as a dump for ash from a bakery, and this, mixed with earth, had built up to a depth of three metres.

The sign for fire shows either a point of glowing fire ending in a tail of smoke or flame rising from a pottery bowl. Excavations at the city of Tell el-Amarna have revealed that kilns for pottery, for making glazed objects and for small-scale metal working, as well as ubiquitous ovens for cooking and baking bread, were dispersed throughout the housing neighbourhoods. Tending fires and obtaining combustible materials must have been a constant chore, and breathing smoky air a regular hazard. Although Egypt is generally a hot country, winter days and especially nights can be quite cold, especially for people living near the desert. A common feature in the central living room of Amarna houses is a broad and shallow pottery bowl, filled with ash and charcoal, set in the floor, often next to a low brick bench. This served as the domestic hearth around which people could gather. In smaller houses the soot-blackened fragments fallen from the mud-plastered ceilings suggest that many poorer people spent part of their indoor lives in smoky atmospheres, too.

With ovens, kilns and small open fires everywhere, lighting a new one was straightforward. Otherwise, Egyptians used a simple friction device, a vertical spindle rotated quickly back and forth in a hollow in a flat piece of wood filled with kindling. A wooden bow with its string looped once around the spindle greatly increased the speed of rotation.

There were times when fires spread out of control. Egyptian settlements contained wood, straw (a common component of mud-bricks), oil, cloth and other inflammable materials. There are some archaeological mounds where large parts have been baked to a red colour through conflagration. This can extend downwards for several metres into the underlying rubble and earth of previous periods, implying that the heat of the fire set off a slow-burning underground fire that would have rendered part of the town uninhabitable for some time. Whether, in individual cases, the cause was accidental or arose from local disturbances is impossible to tell.

The Egyptians believed that the hazardous potential of fire was used by the gods: the sun, and the cobras that were often carved alongside it, gave off fire. Lakes of fire were one of the threats in the Otherworld. Yet the nature of fire, which other cultures have seen as a fundamental element, seems to have excited little or no curiosity among the Egyptians. It had no equivalent to Nun, the primaeval waters, in their thinking about the nature and origin of the material universe.

31. WICK

The standard Egyptian lamp was of the simplest design, a wick lying in a small, shallow bowl. The wick consisted of a narrow strip of old linen twisted from both ends until it naturally doubled back and spiralled upon itself. The word for 'wick' used such a twist as its hieroglyphic determinative sign.

Lamps were not only useful in the house and temple and palace – they were essential for men working underground. In ancient Egypt this mostly meant the making (and also the subsequent robbing) of tombs. The men who cut and decorated the tombs in the Valley of Kings lived in a special village now known as Deir el-Medina in western Thebes. Their lives are documented in remarkable detail on thousands of texts written on pieces of broken pottery or limestone. Some of the texts refer to the lighting materials of the workmen. We learn that wicks were greased with animal fat or soaked in oil (probably sesame oil) in a central depot, hundreds at a time. Bundles of wicks were then parsimoniously handed out to the workmen on the understanding that only a certain number would be used each day, often 32 divided into two sets of 16, probably representing a morning and an afternoon shift. One means of reducing the smoke from an oil lamp is to add salt. Egyptians might have done this as the tombs and their paintings are not disfigured with smoke. One could also coat a wick with incense, and Egyptians lit these in their homes as well as in their temples.

32. CITY

The excavated remains of early towns show them to have been small, irregular in plan and often surrounded by a thick, curving wall which presumably suggested the hieroglyph for a town should be a circle. In the sign the dense network of narrow city streets is reduced to two crossing at right angles. On its own it spells the word 'city', ⬡ *nîwt* (*niwet*), which from the New Kingdom onwards could mean simply Thebes, reflecting Thebes's status as Egypt's ceremonial centre and capital of the south. The hieroglyph also acted as the determinative for 'village', and for the names of individual towns, as in Abydos, ⬡ *ȝbḏw* (*Abdju*); and the proper name of Thebes, ⬡ *Wȝst* (*Waset*). Revealingly it was also used in the writing of the common word for 'Egypt', ⬡ *Kmt* (*Kemet*), implying that the Egyptians regarded their country as fully urbanized, as if one large city. The 'city of eternity' was, of course, the cemetery.

The local city attracted loyalty among its menfolk. A man

boasted of being 'beloved of his city'. On his last journey to the grave he 'came from his city', and his 'city god' held a special place in his affections. The places so called were usually quite small, more like our villages in size. Prior to the New Kingdom they also had little in the way of distinctive public architecture, their modest shrines and official residences made of mud-bricks and set along narrow, cramped streets. The appearance of cities changed in the New Kingdom, when they were freed from the constraints of surrounding walls. They began to spread over larger areas and were, visually and institutionally, taken over by temples, now mostly built of stone and on a large scale. Sacred routes were laid out for temple processions, introducing public spaces and a greater sense of community-wide celebration.

Egyptian cities were still a long way from their modern counterparts. We are used to districts which serve different purposes – residential, manufacturing, shopping, banking, and so on. The largest excavated area of an ancient Egyptian city at Akhenaten's capital at Tell el-Amarna shows little sign of this. Most of the royal buildings lay together in the centre. Otherwise houses of the rich and the poor clustered together into neighbourhoods which appear to have been, to some extent, self-sufficient. The city was like a string of adjoining villages.

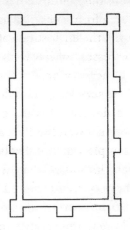

33. WALL

In the pre-modern world, towns and cities were often surrounded by a stout wall, sometimes encouraging a neat rectangular layout of streets within. City walls defended the inhabitants, they marked a clear boundary between where you and your neighbours lived and the more uncertain world outside, and they enabled a check to be kept on who entered and left. For the first half of its history (prior to the New Kingdom), the towns of ancient Egypt were enclosed, either with curving or straight-sided walls. This was useful when local warfare broke out, though it also led to an arms race which had produced wheeled siege-towers by the end of the 3rd millennium BC, one of them depicted in a tomb painting of the period.

By creating a safe zone inside, walls become a symbol of protection. A myth recorded on the walls of the temple of Edfu imagined that, in a primaeval age, the sacred sites of Egypt were the places where the forces of evil in the form of serpents had been defeated by companies of divine beings. According to this myth, temples were then built with a large enclosure wall to protect the sacred area from evils. During the second half of ancient Egyptian history, the enclosure walls around the larger temples resembled fortresses, with towers projecting from the wall faces, and battlements along the top (the temple of Medinet Habu is the best surviving example). The military style was continued on the decorated walls of the temple itself, where large-scale scenes showed the Pharaoh battling his enemies. It was on such temple walls, at Thebes and the Egyptian colonial city of Napata in Sudan, that around 1420 BC King Amenhetep II hung the bodies and severed hands of seven slain princes on his return from warfare in Syria. A model of the enclosure wall around the temple of the god Ptah of Memphis has a human ear carved at the top of each tower, and an accompanying text proclaims that this is 'the place where prayer is heard'. The pious citizen excluded from the temple and stationed outside its ramparts still hoped that his prayers would make their way through and be heard by the god hidden away inside.

Over the same period the walling of towns died away, as far as we can see from the record of excavation, even though Egypt was increasingly exposed to invasion. We have a detailed record of one invasion, by an army led by the Sudanese King Piankhy, around 734 BC. At the city of Hermopolis, 'an embankment was made to enclose the wall. A siege-tower was set up to elevate the archers as they shot, and the slingers as they hurled stones and killed people there each day.' Inside the wall lay the palace and women's quarters of the local prince, and his stables. Piankhy, pointedly ignoring the women after the city's surrender, visits the stables and declares that the prince's worst crime was to let the horses go hungry.

Increasingly the evidence points to the fact that, in these later periods, the large enclosure walls which dotted the Nile floodplain surrounded and protected the temple which lay alongside the unwalled city. These temple enclosure walls also embraced, however, the residences of the leading citizens and their personal assets, which might include their stables (see no. 94, 'Sacred'). These later temple enclosures were, on Egypt's flat plain, each town's citadel.

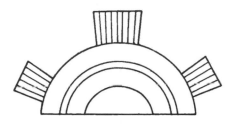

34. MOUND

Show archaeologists a mound rising unexpectedly from the ground and they will think 'ancient site?'. Places long settled become mounds simply because, in the past, as dust and rubbish accumulated in the streets of towns and cities, the ground level gradually rose, and people often rebuilt their houses over the ruins of the old. When Egypt was mapped in 1798, by surveyors accompanying Napoleon's armies, grass-covered earthy mounds, sometimes hundreds of metres long, dotted the Egyptian land scape, each one containing a layered history of habitation. Some still survive, but mostly beneath the modern towns of Egypt's burgeoning population. They were a feature of the ancient land-scape, too. A surveyor who made a record of farmlands in the reign of Rameses V made frequent use of local landmarks, and among them were mounds.

Drawing upon a different tradition of knowledge, Egyptians also believed mounds to hold ancient secrets. Mounds on the floodplain could be places where the gods first made their home and set about the task of creation. The library of the Ptolemaic temple of Edfu included a 'specification of the mounds of the first primaeval age', which would have been an annotated list of the sacred places – later chosen as the temple sites. Traces in the foundations suggest some were built on artificial mounds. This architectural ritual had a counterpart in mounds built over the burial chambers of tombs in the early dynasties. The square flat-topped construction concealed within the Step Pyramid of King Djoser at Sakkara is perhaps the most elaborate example.

Three small triangles representing trees sit above the hieroglyph. Although the word for 'mound', $\overset{\frown}{\mathsf{I}}{}_{\mathsf{\small\Omega}}$ (iȝt) yat, could mean a ruin, which would naturally support vegetation, the trees also symbolized the re-emergent life that grew out of the entombed body of the god Osiris. In his story of murder and resurrection the Egyptians saw hope of their own resurrection after death. The link between temple mounds and Osiris grew to be ubiquitous. Each nome in Egypt contained its own tree-covered mound in recognition of this spiritual belief. The concept inspired a remarkable piece of architecture (known as the Osireion) at Abydos, a desert site in Upper Egypt where the tomb of Osiris was thought to be. In the grounds of his temple, King Seti I (1294–1279 BC) built an artificial tree-covered mound beneath which, in a great chamber cut into the desert, lay a place of burial. It had the form of an island surrounded by a moat – a channel kept filled with water from an underground conduit – recreating the primaeval mound where life had first appeared.

35. WEST

The daily passage of the sun and nightly rotation of the stars gave the Egyptians an east and a west, and the course of the Nile a south and a north. Ancient Egyptians' overall sense of orientation was similar to ours, except that they positioned their viewpoint as if they were facing towards the south (see no. 43, 'Boat'), so that the word for 'west' was also that for 'right hand'.

Lying west of Egypt was a foreign land of desert and oases where dwelt a traditional enemy of Egypt, the Libyans, whom the Egyptians typecast as wearing a single ostrich-feather in their hair. After successful large-scale immigration in the late New Kingdom (c. 1200–1000 BC) the Libyans became Egypt's ruling elite for several generations. They provided the kings of the 22nd Dynasty, adapting themselves to Egyptian ways, although we have no testimony as to what native Egyptians thought of this.

The west also had a mythical existence. It was the realm of the dead, where the imaginary 'Field of Offerings' was to be found. Mourners who dragged funeral sledges would cry 'To the West, to the West, the sweet land of life!' It was presided over by the 'Foremost of the Westerners', a jackal-god pre-eminent at Abydos in the Old Kingdom, who later (by the early Middle Kingdom, c. 2050 BC) developed into an epithet for the great king of the dead, Osiris (see no. 39, 'Jackal').

The hieroglyph for the west shows a standard with a rounded top from which two ribbons hang and to which is fixed, at a slight angle, the same ostrich feather as adorns the heads of Libyans. The practice of making standards of this kind began in the prehistoric period, as we know from pictures of them on pottery jars and other objects. This was so long in the past for the Egyptians of the historic periods that, if one were able now to ask them what meaning lay behind these standards and this hieroglyph in particular, it is quite likely that they would either not know or would give an answer that was not historically accurate. In standing for the realm of the dead as well as for the west generally the hieroglyph was incorporated into the symbolism of resurrection. It could be interpreted as a goddess, wearing the standard like a crown, who welcomes the dead.

In prehistoric times the dead were normally laid on their left side, knees flexed towards the chest, and with their head to the south. In this position the dead faced the west. During the Old Kingdom, however, the body position gradually changed. Laying out the dead prone and on their backs was preferred (the model for this was the mummified body of Osiris), with their head to the north. Coffins were decorated with a pair of eyes towards the head end, but facing east, the direction of the rising sun. The rich variety of the Egyptians' beliefs, which were never codified into a single system, left them with many choices, and it is hard for us to say why one burial method was preferred over another.

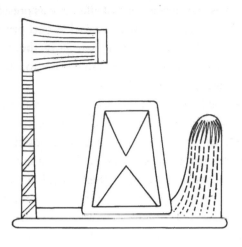

36. CEMETERY

The Egyptians believed that the ideal location for a cemetery lay in the western desert, a place of haunting emptiness, where it was easier to imagine a spirit world and where the jackals lived. One word, ⚊ *smyt (semit)*, meant both 'cemetery' and 'desert'. The hieroglyph chosen here, ⚊ , writes the commonest word for cemetery which means literally 'god's portion'. It combines a picture of the desert hillside (see no. 2, 'Desert') with the hieroglyph which writes the word 'to be divine' (see no. 93, 'Divine'). For those in the Nile delta, however, and even for many who lived in the valley itself, the cemetery was a patch of uncultivated ground not far outside the town and not necessarily on the west side. In parts of Egypt, cliffs on the eastern side of the river were more easily carved into rock tombs, and the famous tombs at Beni Hasan are a testimony to this pragmatic choice.

Officials – local community leaders and provincial governors – were a small but significant portion of ancient Egyptian society who administered the country on behalf of the king (see no. 80, 'Official'). Many inherited a place in a family tomb, but a man setting out to make a mark for himself was likely to want to make his own tomb. This would have involved decisions with a lifetime of implications. Did a man see himself as primarily a courtier and so seek to place his tomb in the cemetery close to a royal residence city, even beside the tomb of his king, or did his heart remain with his birthplace in a country town where perhaps the bulk of his estates lay and where his tomb would become a local landmark?

A man could sink a fortune into his tomb. He could insist on carved stone rather than painted bricks, requiring years of part-time labour by skilled sculptors, probably loaned from the court circles. He would need at least one statue for himself, perhaps several, and one for his wife. If his burial place was in Upper Egypt, where the desert rose in a cliff or a steep slope, he could have the whole edifice carved out of the rock and then decorated. Many tombs remained unfinished by the time death intervened.

A tomb did more than proclaim a successful life. It was the centre of a parallel household; a spiritual household which depended in part on the support and services of the living. In death an Egyptian became a minor god, requiring regular offerings of food, the performance of temple-like rituals and the observance of festivals. All of this was paid for by setting up, through deeds of conveyance or agreements with the king, what we now see as a charitable foundation. Income from land was secured, and paid to priests to perform regular services. Ideally priests would be members of the family, under the leadership of the eldest son, who would be guaranteed an income for life as a 'mortuary priest'. Some landowners seem to have tied up a large part of their estates in this way, so securing it for their descendants.

Thoughtful Egyptians recognized the vanity involved in building lasting monuments. A poem in praise of being a scribe contrasts the longevity of a wise man's reputation with the decay of grand tombs:

Their portals and mansions have crumbled, their mortuary priests have gone; their tombstones are covered with dirt, their graves are forgotten. Their name is pronounced through their writings which they made whilst they were yet alive.

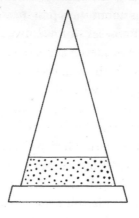

37. PYRAMID

Imagine that you are an ancient Egyptian on your way to visit Memphis, the original capital of your country. As you approach your journey's end you see, on the distant low desert horizon to the west, the pale triangular profiles of pyramids. By the end of the era of royal pyramid building around 1700 BC, some 15 pyramids would have been conspicuous up to the north of Memphis, and another 15 to the south, over a combined distance of some 35 kilometres, with isolated outliers even further to the south. If you had a little learning you might know the names of some of the royal owners: King Sneferu of good repute; cruel and impious King Khufu, who had built the largest pyramid of all (the Great Pyramid); perhaps Djoser, a king of a very distant time indeed (his was the Step Pyramid); and even Userkaf and his two twin brothers whose mother, according to legend, had been the wife of a priest of the sun-god and his father the sun-god Ra himself. You might even know the names of some of the pyramids: 'Sneferu Endures' or 'The Perfection of Pepi is

Established', ⊗ △ ⌐ ╿ ═ 〖ΠΒ〗 (*Pepy men-nefer*) (the abbreviated version of this one has given us the name Memphis).

Egyptians, curious about their past, visited old monuments. One of the sons of Rameses II, Khaemwese, the high-priest of the god Ptah of Memphis, even supervised restorations of several of the pyramids which were now a thousand years old. If, out of interest and respect, you crossed the fields from Memphis and climbed the desert to visit one of the pyramids, you would find yourself faced not only with the towering mass of the pyramid itself, but with a veritable 'city' around its base. In a prominent position stood the decorated stone temple where, generations after the king had died, priests were still paid to offer food and drink to his spirit and to look after the ritual equipment kept in storerooms. Over the adjacent ground spread networks of tombs for those who had served the king. They, too, had left means to pay for the upkeep of their cult. Gradually, of course, the cults slipped into oblivion, but for a time people would come and go, or dwell among the tombs in mud-brick shanties. Some visitors were drawn to leave their own memorials, in the form of graffiti. One scribe, on visiting the temple for King Sneferu's pyramid, remarked that 'he found it like heaven within when the sun-god is rising in it', despite its small size and lack of decoration.

It is still not clear why Egyptians chose to build monuments in a pyramid shape. The first (belonging to King Djoser of the 3rd Dynasty, c. 2660 BC) was stepped and unpointed. Where masonry at the bottom has fallen away you can see that, to begin with, Djoser's tomb had been covered with a single flat-topped platform of stone which may have simply marked the location and provided a place for offerings but might also have represented a place of resurrection (see no. 34, 'Mound'). Before the king died, his architect, growing more confident with experience, aimed for much greater height and achieved it by building what was, in effect, a series of six platforms one on top of the other. This is the most direct explanation, but particular images might also have been in his mind, such as a giant staircase to the heavens.

Later pyramids were smooth with pointed peaks. Centuries after Djoser, ancient Egyptians would have connected the idea of a pyramid with the rising sun and with a sacred standing-stone at the city of Heliopolis, a centre of the cult of the sun-god Ra. The name of this stone, *benben*, gave rise to a word for the pointed stone at the very top of pyramids, *benbent*. Earlier pyramids were uninscribed but in the Middle Kingdom the sides of the pointed capstone were carved with short prayers to the rising sun.

Despite its singular shape and power as a religious image, the pyramid had ceased by the New Kingdom to mark the royal tomb. Kings now chose instead to be buried in discrete underground chambers in the Valley of Kings at Thebes, their cult separately situated in a temple of conventional design.

38. MUMMY

The bodies of the dead rapidly decompose. Cremation or excarnation (exposing the corpse until only clean bones remain, widely practised, for example, in Neolithic Europe) deals with decomposition directly; burial in the ground hides it from view. The ancient Egyptians, like their ancient African neighbours and prehistoric predecessors, chose burial. In the dry warm desert burial quickly brings decomposition to a halt and natural mummification takes place, leaving a shrivelled but recognizable version of the original person; but many Egyptian cemeteries, especially those in the delta, were in relatively damp soil and bodies must have been reduced to skeletons, the bones turning soft, within a few years.

The Egyptians wrote long religious texts about the dead. Some passages sought to ensure that the dead remained in possession of the principal parts of their body. One means was by associating each body part with a god. So Chapter 42 of the Book of the Dead states: 'My hair is Nun, my face is Ra, my eyes are

Hathor . . . my feet are Ptah, my toes are living falcons. There is
no member of mine devoid of a god. Thoth is the protection of all
my flesh.' As the cult of Osiris expanded late in the Old Kingdom,
the ideal shape for the dead was that of Osiris, back and legs in a
stiff straight line and the whole body tightly swathed in linen,
except for the hands which remained free to grasp certain
symbols.

The Egyptians developed a process of artificial mummification to preserve body tissue and key organs (the brain was not
considered important, and was removed in pieces through the
nasal cavity). The powdered mineral natron (see no. 3, 'Grain')
was heaped over the body to dry the tissue; a similar substance can
be made by mixing cooking salt with bicarbonate of soda. If a
piece of meat is buried in it for some days it becomes dry and
hard, and shrivels. The Egyptians disguised the shrivelling of the
body by extensively wrapping it in linen strips. Organs (liver, stomach, intestines, lungs and heart) were removed through an incision
in the side of the body, desiccated and wrapped separately. The
organs were then buried in a set of four special 'canopic' jars,
with the exception of the heart, which ideally was returned to the
body cavity. The whole process, if properly carried out, involved
purification ceremonies, the application of coats of resin to the
body, and finally, possibly at the time of interment, the 'Opening
of the Mouth' ritual, by which the mummified body was made
ready to receive prayers and offerings. According to one text of the
New Kingdom 70 days was the proper duration for all of this.

Mummification was a skilled and time-consuming process
which many could not afford. The burials of poorer people were
less protected from processes of decay, so that archaeologists find
it difficult to be sure to what extent such bodies were mummified
at all and so cannot tell what proportion of the population was
mummified after death. The early history of mummification is
also not well documented, and the various stages in the process
might not have developed at the same time. King Djer of the 1st
Dynasty had his limbs wrapped in linen, but the first evidence for
the removal of organs for separate preservation is the presence,

four centuries later, of special 'canopic' containers in the tomb of Queen Hetep-heres. The use of natron, however, is perhaps older than the 1st Dynasty.

Ironically, by burying valuables in tombs, the Egyptians greatly increased the risk of disturbance of the dead. A papyrus confession of robbers on trial in the 16th year of Rameses IX (1110 BC) reports how, equipped with heavy bronze chisels and lamps, the thieves broke into the burial chamber of King Sebekemsaf II and his Queen Nubkhaas, whose tomb had remained undisturbed for nearly five centuries. 'The noble mummy of this king was entirely covered with gold and his coffins were adorned with gold and silver, inside and out, and inlaid with all kinds of precious stones.' Having stripped off everything of value, they set fire to the coffins and the bodies inside. The gold totalled 160 *deben*, a weight equivalent to 14.56 kilograms. It represented the value of, say, a herd of 250 cattle according to ancient Egyptian prices, and so offered the allure of transforming a poor man's life (see no. 87, 'Gold').

39. JACKAL

Prominent among Egyptian images of death is a dog-like animal, often called Anubis. But at Abydos, a holy site on the desert edge in Upper Egypt, the animal is called 'The Foremost of the Westerners' (*Khenty-amentiu*). 'Jackal' is a modern translation but Egyptian images merged the characteristics of jackals, dogs and foxes. All scavenge on the desert margins, are frequently nocturnal and must in the past have found convenient homes in the deserted cemeteries. Jackals also emit an unearthly howling cry.

Anubis was a central figure in the Egyptian afterlife. He assisted Osiris in the Hall of Judgement to which the dead would first be conducted. He presided over the process of mummification, being often called 'the one in the place of embalming'. And as a recumbent canine, sometimes coloured black, he guarded the tomb.

Egyptians were impressed by jackals' navigational skills over desert tracks. In mythology a group of four towed the heavenly barque of the sun-god. The city of Asyut was the cult centre for yet another canine god called Wep-wawet, whose name means 'Opener of the Ways'. The main festival at Abydos saw a procession set out across the desert from the temple to the tomb of Osiris, at its head an image of Wep-wawet to 'open the way'. People set up small memorial stones in the adjacent desert, some carved with short prayers and even tiny windows, which express a wish to see Wep-wawet and his procession.

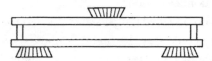

40. ROAD

Although the river Nile provided a fine means of travel from one part of the country to another, many journeys were made by land either on foot or on the back of a donkey, in a carrying chair or even by a wheeled vehicle. One hieroglyph depicts a length of road or track with borders on which grow trees or clumps of vegetation. It writes the word $\overset{\leftrightarrow}{\underset{\triangle}{\shortmid}}$ *w3t (wat)* which means both the 'road' on which one treads and the 'way' of doing something. To 'open a way' is similar to the English 'make one's way'. It has the added meaning of removing obstacles from one's path, rather like the English 'make way for', and was associated with the god Wepwawet, 'opener of the ways'.

We know almost nothing of land routes within ancient Egypt. We can assume that dirt tracks linked towns and villages, but whether kings initiated a road system, especially in later centuries when horse and chariot were common, we cannot tell. A picture of land travel and its dangers is provided by the story of a poor countryman, named Khun-anup, making his long way to market with his laden donkey. He takes a path between the riverbank and a field of barley. An unscrupulous agent of a rich man lays a linen cloth across the path. While the poor countryman protests at the blocking of his way, his donkey turns his head and eats a little of the barley, providing the agent with the excuse he was seeking to confiscate the donkey.

For those who travelled long distances on land, were there hostels where they could stay the night? A manual of advice by the sage Ankhsheshonk (late 1st millennium BC) argues against simply knocking on people's doors: 'Do not stay on the road till evening, saying "I am sure of the houses." You do not know the hearts of their inhabitants.'

41. DONKEY

One will look in vain for a hieroglyph of a camel. Camels were latecomers to Egypt and were apparently not used even by the Egyptians' desert neighbours. The donkey was the universal beast of burden, carrying loads on tracks between villages and fields, and on long journeys outside Egypt. The big landowners kept them by the hundred. Around 2250 BC an expedition leader, Harkhuf, based at Aswan, recorded his return from a trading mission to Nubia. With him were 300 donkeys laden with exotic goods.

The stubbornness of donkeys was as evident to ancient Egyptians as it is to us today. To express what they saw as the donkey's malign character, Egyptians associated the donkey with the god Seth, and sometimes wrote the word with the special determinative of Seth, ⟨hieroglyphs⟩ ꜥꜣ (a'a, perhaps in imitation of a donkey's bray).

Donkeys were equally at home in Palestine, and a surviving Egyptian picture shows a tribal leader riding one. For a time in the

late Middle Kingdom and in the subsequent century when northern Egypt was ruled by Palestinian kings called the Hyksos (see
no. 2, 'Desert'), Palestinian families made their homes in the eastern delta. Beside their tombs they cut separate pits for the burial
of donkeys and also sheep, a custom they had brought with them.
It is probable that the animals were sacrificed at the time of burial.

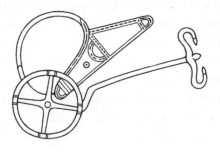

42. CHARIOT

The earliest evidence of the wheel in Egypt is found in pictures of siege warfare in the 6th Dynasty and 1st Intermediate Period (c. 2300/2050 BC), where wheels are seen fixed to the bottom of a scaling ladder or a siege-tower. Evidence of the wheel is so rare that we do not even know what word ancient Egyptians used for 'wheel' prior to the New Kingdom. We cannot judge, therefore, how widespread wheeled transport was. In the New Kingdom, when the evidence increases a little, both spoked and solid wheels appear in pictures and models of four- and six-wheeled wagons, the former sometimes used to bear coffins. It was presumably on vehicles of this kind that King Tuthmosis III transported his fleet of riverboats across Syria for a campaign on the river Euphrates against the kingdom of Mitanni, a remarkable feat only briefly mentioned in his annals.

By the beginning of the New Kingdom the Egyptians had adopted the two-wheeled chariot from their Near Eastern neighbours, whose better equipped armies the Egyptians now faced up to more determinedly than before. They needed two horses, one on either side of a central pole, and to maintain stability over rough ground, they had their lightly built wheels widely set on a long axle. The chariot became the key instrument of warfare and symbolized the vigour and bravery of the king (and his courtiers) both in hunting and in warfare.

To possess a chariot was to join a social elite. The upkeep of horses and chariots needed specialist support. Their introduction and use gave rise to a whole new professional group, the 'stable masters', a new technical vocabulary, and the development of skills needed to build and maintain the ancient equivalent of our racing car.

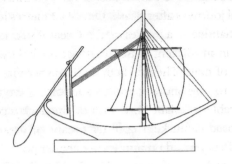

43. BOAT, TRAVELLING UPSTREAM

Ease of transport along the Nile encouraged Egypt to develop into an integrated society. Officials of the Pharaoh constantly travelled between the court and the provinces carrying detailed instructions and reports, controlling the country and its resources. Most people did not have to travel very far to catch a boat. Even today the edge of the floodplain in Upper Egypt is never more than 20 kilometres from the river, and in ancient times this would have been less, with many of the towns and cities close to the riverbank. In the delta the Nile conveniently divided into several branches (now reduced to two) which brought many cities on that broad flat plain within reach of water transport. Boats and barges carried farmers and kings, armies and scribes, the annual harvest and giant loads of stone. The Colossi of Memnon, each one 18 metres high and made from a single block of a particularly dense stone, quartzite, must have been floated down to Thebes on immense barges from the quarries 200 kilometres to the south.

Rich men owned many boats, for fishing, for pleasure, for carrying their harvest, and for journeying longer distances, with separate boats for servants and for a travelling kitchen.

Full-sized boats were buried beside the pyramids of kings for use in special journeys after death. One, 43.3 metres long, was discovered dismantled in a pit beside the Great Pyramid and is now reassembled in an adjacent museum. It was not built with a keel or with the use of nails. The hull kept its shape because the timbers were lashed to one another and to supporting wooden frames using thick cables of plant fibre. Part of the deck is covered with a long enclosed cabin kept cool by means of a second, outer wooden roof supported on numerous slender poles.

Boats, like today, were named. 'The Wild Bull', 'The Northern' and 'Arising in Memphis' were successive boats of the Nile battle fleet of Thebes in which an officer, Ahmose of El-Kab, served during the war against the Hyksos. 'Strong of Prow is Amun' was the grand state barge which conveyed the statue of the god Amun on feast days.

The hieroglyph for 'boat' indicates the normal method for steering. At the stern stood a long pole lashed to a vertical post, with a tiller at the top and a broad rudder at the bottom. By rotating the pole and the rudder the ship was steered. Larger boats were provided with a pair of poles, one on either side of the stern. The hieroglyph also shows the sail up, filled with the wind that generally blows from the north. In this version it acted as a determinative in the word  (*ḫntỉ*) (*khenti*), meaning 'to travel south', even when the journey was on foot or when the movement was the passage of the north wind itself. When the Egyptian army crossed Syria in the 18th Dynasty and came to the Euphrates, which contrary to the Nile flows southwards, they described the river as 'flowing downstream in an upstream direction'. To the Egyptians the direction upstream was evidently the natural 'front' of the country so that the word for travelling south was really 'to advance'. West meant right (see no. 35, 'West'), east meant left, and the northern marshy part of the country was the 'rear',  *pḥww* (*pehwy*). This word was the same as that for the rump of an animal and (as a feminine noun) for 'rectum'. There is a good case for drawing maps of ancient Egypt with north at the bottom.

Another version of the hieroglyph, ⛵, dispenses with the mast, which could be lowered to lie flat on the deck. This version serves as the normal determinative for a range of words for 'boat' and for related activities, such as 'to sail', and more particularly 'to sail (or rather drift) downstream', ⛵ ⚓ *ḥdỉ* (*khedi*), with the implication that this was often done with the mast down to take advantage of the northward current. By this word the Egyptians expressed the more general sense of travelling northwards, not necessarily by the river. The same sign inverted is a vivid determinative for the verb ⛵ ⚓ *pnꜥ* (*pena*), 'to overturn'.

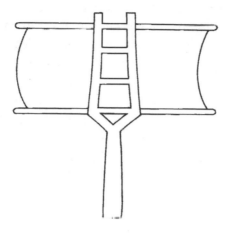

44. SAIL

The hieroglyph depicts the sail of a boat filled with wind. It acts as the determinative for the noun 'sail'. It is also the principal sign used to write the word 'wind', and many passages of text show that the same word, identically spelt, means 'breath', from the mouth and from the nose. The 'sweet breath of life' was the gift of kings and gods. Its opposite, 'the breath of an outside-god or death', is mentioned in a medical papyrus as a cause of sickness.

The sign is the common determinative for words for particular kinds of wind, among which are four named after the cardinal points: 'north wind', 'east wind', 'west wind' and 'south wind'. In Egypt, the wind can blow bitterly cold from the north, and stiflingly hot from the south, in both cases whipping up dust storms. The steady cooling breeze from the north tempers the heat of the summer and early autumn. The 'sweet breath of the north wind' was requested in prayers for the afterlife. Ancient Egyptian houses were sometimes designed to take the greatest advantage of this breeze, either through a north-facing portico which looked out to a garden or by means of a roof ventilator above a bedroom which funnelled the northerly breeze down onto the sleeping occupant below.

45. SACRED BARQUE

Boats were the vehicles of the gods. They were by far the largest manufactured objects and suggested movement on a far grander, cosmic scale than, say, chariots. The Egyptians envisaged the sun as a voyager across the sky. In a boat with an upward-curving prow and sickle-shaped stern, they depicted the sun-god standing within a central canopy with a curved roof supported on slender posts shaped like papyrus plants. For the special moments of sunrise and sunset artists depicted two versions of the barque, each with distinctive additional symbols. At night, and towed by ropes, this barque continued its journey through the cavernous dangers of the Otherworld (see no. 47).

No temple seems to have been complete without at least one scaled-down boat fit for the temple gods. A god's statue sat in a central cabin, sometimes half-hidden behind a veil of linen. Overlaid with gold leaf and provided with decorative additions, these godly vehicles were carried on the shoulders of priests in religious processions. They were the work of master craftsmen. One such man, a chief of goldsmiths of the reign of Rameses II named Nakht-djehuty, 'obeyed the call' to make portable barques for various gods, perhaps as many as 26. Another craftsman, the shipbuilder Iuna of the reign of Tuthmosis IV, built barques for 14 deities. One of the barques, for Osiris, had its own name, Neshmet, and was repeatedly re-made or replaced. It was carried across the desert at Abydos and was the ritual centrepiece, where priests repelled the enemies of Osiris. The most elaborate was the barque named Henu, fitted at the prow with a fan of projecting wooden stays displaying animal, fish and bird heads, the preserve of the god Sokar of Memphis. This was dragged or carried around the walls of the city on his feast days.

Temple processions, on religious feast days or public celebrations, followed a route outside the temple enclosure, which would have been paved and flanked with sphinxes. The Festival of Opet at Thebes saw the portable barques of the three gods, Amun, Mut and Khensu, carried to the river's edge from their home in Karnak temple and then loaded onto a huge boat, also gilded and decorated. This was towed by the citizens of Thebes for the short distance to Luxor temple, where the portable barques were unloaded and carried into the temple for the culminating ceremonies which spiritually renewed the reigning king. On a smaller scale, the villagers of Deir el-Medina, workmen for the neighbouring necropolis, carried a barque containing an unshrouded statue of their founder, King Amenhetep I, around the outside of the village walls. Villagers presented the statue with petitions which the king would supposedly answer by movements of the barque as it rested on the shoulders of the bearers, or even by a speech read out by an attendant scribe (see no. 97, 'Wonder').

46. SKY

A flat line with downward-pointing peaks at either end conveys the arching nature of the sky. More detailed hieroglyphic drawings include stars (as here); the Egyptians conceived of the sky as it appears at night. The dark starry sky was the background against which the sun-god and his attendants journeyed (see no. 47, 'Otherworld'). To this extent, 'sky' deserves the translation 'heaven'. It was not, however, the kingdom of Osiris or a paradise for the dead, the Egyptians holding in their minds several parallel visions of the afterlife and abode of the gods.

An elongated version of the hieroglyph was carved above scenes on temple walls, symbolizing the proximity that temples had to heaven. The dark blue night sky with a pattern of yellow stars was the common design for ceilings above sacred spaces – the rooms in temples and the burial chambers of kings. In the burial chambers the hieroglyph was sometimes transformed into the goddess Nût, the downward-pointing ends of the sign becoming her arms and legs as she arched herself across the sky. The Egyptians also believed that the sky rested upon four 'supports' which held it aloft, each one a pole, v-shaped at the top.

Night was a fearful time: 'Earth is in darkness as if in death. One sleeps in chambers, heads covered. One eye does not see another. Were they robbed of their goods, that are under their heads, people would not notice it. Every lion comes from its den. All the serpents bite.' It was a time for robbery, assault and assassination. In a fictional account of King Amenemhat's life, he describes his fated murder: 'It was after supper, night had come. I was taking an hour of rest, lying on my bed, for I was weary. As my heart began to follow sleep, weapons for my protection were turned against me . . . No one is strong at night; no one can fight alone.'

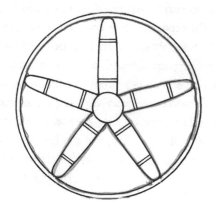

47. OTHERWORLD (DUAT)

A whole religious mythology developed around the disappearance of the sun during the night, when Egyptians believed it travelled back from west to east through a realm called Duat, or Dat, which can be translated as 'Otherworld'. Duat was considered a real place alongside heaven, earth, water and mountains. Its hieroglyph shows a star (see no. 48) set within a circle which presumably expresses the entire realm of the night sky.

Egyptians regarded Duat as an opaque medium in which the sun passed overhead unseen from earth. One myth suggested that the slim naked goddess, Nût, who arched over the earth and on whose body the stars were fixed, swallowed the sun as it was setting. It then passed through her body to be born again the following morning. Within this opaque tunnel was the world of gates and gatekeepers, winding waterways sometimes of fire, enemies in torment, serpents and caverns – these details were further elaborated over the centuries. The dead accessed Duat through 'the secret portals of the west'.

Maps of Duat were painted in the rock tombs of the Valley of Kings. They have various titles, 'Book of What Is in the Duat', 'Book of Gates', 'Book of Caverns', 'Book of Breathings'. Their contents overlap and their deeper significance is often hard to fathom. Part of the ancient interest lay in filling out the imaginary details of the place and its occupants. From the prominence given to these depictions and the care devoted to their details we can judge them as serious intellectual speculations of the priestly elite. The journeys through Duat suggest a belief in constant cycles of resurrection, and possibly an attempt to define the turmoil that seems always to lie beneath the visible world, Duat being a place of enemies who had to be subdued by the sun-god.

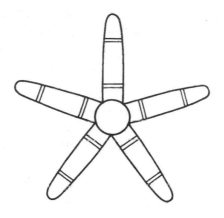

48. STAR

The Egyptian night sky is an astronomer's dream. In the clear air, even when there is no moon, it is so brightly lit with stars that one can dimly make out tracks in the desert. Yet although the ancient Egyptians have a reputation for being good astronomers their interest was not primarily in mapping the heavens. Instead, they preferred to map the invented Otherworld, and stars were worked into patterns to aid the measurement of time or in a manner that was not primarily observational. They named certain constellations and bright stars – for example, Orion – the northern circumpolar stars, and the bright star Sirius ($\overset{\ominus}{\ast}$ $\triangle$ *Spdt* (*Sepdet*), who was also the goddess Sepdet, 'mistress of the New Year'). It is generally accepted that the pyramids of the Old Kingdom were aligned to the north using the positions of a pair of faint stars, then the closest to the north point of the heavens (the position now occupied by the Pole Star). The hieroglyph of a five-pointed star surrounding a tiny circle, which is its point of light, writes the word for 'star'.

In paintings and texts, stars were the fixed background across which the sun and moon journeyed. Nonetheless, the Egyptians measured the passage of time during the night by the rising and setting of stars. Using pictorial tables ('star clocks') and a simple sighting instrument they were able to divide the night into 12 equal periods. The word for these periods, ⚹ ⊙ ☲ *wnwt* (*wenut*), in effect 'hour', regularly has the star hieroglyph as its determinative, often accompanied by the sign of the sun's disc standing for 'day' or simply 'time'. It belongs to a family of similarly written words which include 'the one who is on the hour', thus 'star watcher' or 'hour watcher', the nearest Egyptian word to 'astronomer'; a word meaning 'priesthood', or 'staff' or 'workers' more generally; and another with the meaning 'duty' or 'service'. The star clocks were similar to the zodiac, although they recognized 36 rather than 12 divisions of the night sky. The Egyptians, however, did not develop astrology. The zodiac comes from Babylonia and was taken up only under the Greek-speaking successors of Alexander the Great. Modern visitors to the temple at Dendera, built at this time, can see an Egyptian version of the zodiac on the temple ceiling, but it does not represent something rooted in Egypt's ancient past.

By the New Kingdom the hours of the day were being measured as well, either by a shadow clock or by a water clock (clepsydra), a basin with internal graduations from which water slowly trickled. The Egyptians did not add the hours of the day and night together to create a single 24-hour series, so they needed tables to list the unequal division of hours of day and night through the year, month by month. During the first month of the year, for example, the day had 16 hours and the night eight.

The measurement of hourly time helped regulate temple ritual, but it seems not to have mattered to people generally. Texts about daily life make no use of time subdivided into 'hours'. Nor do the various transcripts of court cases. People high and low probably lived according to their self-regulating body clocks.

49. YEAR

Before the completion of the high dam at Aswan in 1970, each year
was marked by the rise of Nile waters in the late summer and the
inundation of the floodplain (see no. 8, 'Water'), an event celebrated
in the pre-Islamic calendar as the new year. It roughly coincided
with the yearly reappearance just before dawn of a particularly bright
star, Sirius. The ancient Egyptians divided the ensuing year into three
seasons – the 'inundation', 'growing' and 'fallow' – each four months
long. Each month was exactly 30 days long, leaving five days over in
the year. They called this interval 'the five days extra to the year' and
celebrated it with feast days (see no. 95, 'Festival'). Yet a year of 365
days is slightly too short to keep pace with the movement of the
earth, which we now compensate for with the addition of an extra
day in every fourth year. Very slowly the administrative year of pre-
cisely 365 days, because it lacked a leap year, fell behind the natural
year, passing through a cycle of divergence and then convergence
over the course of 1460 years. The Egyptians recognized and took

account of this shifting calendar. Around 1864 BC a priest noted the coming feast of the first rising of Sirius, which marked the beginning of the agricultural year. He dated it by reference to the administrative calendar which, by this time, had fallen significantly out of step with the agricultural year, despite the retention of the old names for the seasons. The precise date of his note is the sixteenth day of the fourth month of the growing season (in the seventh year of the reign of King Senusret III), revealing a discrepancy of 226 days between the natural and administrative calendars. From this piece of information we can calculate the date in terms of our own Christian era dating.

Scribes followed the progress of the calendar and knew the date of the current day by keeping daily journals of work done. The hieroglyph for 'year' depicts a notched central rib from a palm leaf, with a curving top. Mostly the hieroglyphic form simplifies the notches into a single marker, thus ⌐. No example of such a tally has been found, but it would have been a simple means of keeping account of the days that had passed since the beginning of the year for the majority of the population who were not scribes.

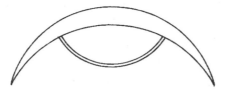

50. MOON

The hieroglyph shows the crescent moon or a combination of the faintly visible full disc of the moon and its illuminated crescent. The Egyptians followed the moon's course carefully, creating a separate monthly calendar to regulate temple festivals and giving to each of its 30 days a separate name. Each of the lunar months also had its own name. The monthly cycle began the day after the moon showed no illuminated segment of itself. The first and thinnest crescent heralded the second day, known as 'new crescent day', the last day was known as 'the procession of Min', a god of fertility whose home was the city of Coptos.

The moon was a divine being, Iah. For a while 'Iah' was popular in personal names among the Egyptian people and the first king of the 18th Dynasty (and thus of the New Kingdom), was named Iahmes or Ahmes ('The moon is born'). Although there are no known temples dedicated to the god Iah, the moon was featured above the heads of two major gods, though it is debatable whether either can be properly called a moon-god. One was Khensu, a god of Thebes (and the son of Amun-Ra). As a Ptolemaic text puts it: '[Khensu] is conceived on the first day of the lunar month, is born on the second day, and grows old after the fifteenth day.' The other was Thoth, normally shown as an ibis or a baboon, and patron of learning and languages. Neither god, nor any other manifestation of the moon, is the subject of surviving myths, however, and we can deduce that the moon held a relatively minor place in Egyptian thinking.

51. ETERNITY

Egyptian numerals were a little like Roman numerals, using different signs for units up to nine, for tens, hundreds, thousands, ten thousands, hundred thousands and finally millions (although practical calculations hardly ever ventured into multiples at the higher end of the scale). The word for 'million', ꒐ *ḥḥ* (*heh*), is a hieroglyph of a squatting man raising his arms in an expansive gesture and bearing on his head, or in each hand, a notched palm-rib, the symbol for 'year'. The word stood for an inordinately large number, made even more emphatic by repetition, 'millions upon millions'. It particularly referred to years and came to mean 'eternity'. The man became Heh, the spirit of eternity.

The Egyptians tended to use the term when referring to a king's eternal power. Eternity stretched into the future, an endless repetition of the prosperous years that they liked to think was the norm. They did recognize, however, that calamities could strike their country. In one tale a learned man, Neferti, is summoned to entertain the king (Sneferu, of the 4th Dynasty) and offers him the choice of hearing about the past or the future. When the king chooses the latter Neferti describes a time of calamity, in which society has collapsed and all the normal marks of civilized behaviour have been turned on their head. A strong king will then restore order. The tale was written five centuries after King Sneferu's death and the time of healing was in fact taking place. It is one of a number of texts which suggest a historic time was viewed as an alternation between times of order and disorder.

Egyptians also recognized the eternity of the divine world, found in the Otherworld. In one myth the goddess of the sky, Nût, becomes a cow, the stars spread across her belly. When Nût begins to tremble on account of her great height above the earth, the sun-god Ra creates eight 'eternity' gods whose upraised arms will support her and thus the weight of the sky, acknowledging its eternal nature. The Otherworld's darker forces were also blessed with eternal life. Serpents forever bite their own tails, their long bodies curving round to form a circle, symbolizing endless time.

The Egyptians believed that eternal existence after death was available to all, and that the chances of achieving it were increased by knowing what to say at the appropriate time. The Book of the Dead was a particularly popular source of words of power. In Chapter 42 a dead person states: 'I am yesterday; one who views a million years; my name is one who passes on the paths of those who are in charge of destinies. I am the lord of eternity.'

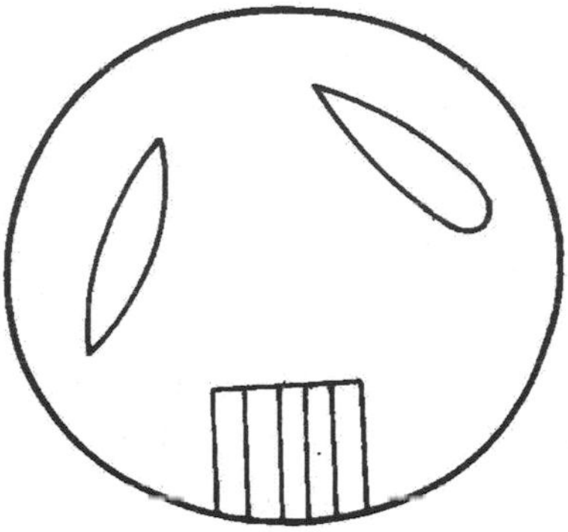

52. PRIMAEVAL TIME

The sign for primaeval time was chosen because of its phonetic similarity to a word for bread. It shows a flat round loaf,  *pꜣt* (*pat*), pinched on the upper surface and used particularly in temple offerings. The primaeval age was a remote past time, when the gods had ruled the world, prior to the well-documented reigns of Egyptian kings. The longest record of kings that has survived, written on a papyrus around 1250 BC in the time of Rameses II, contained at least 250 names of kings and the exact length of their reign, interspersed with summaries of how long a particular group of kings had occupied the throne. Despite several missing sections in the document, we know it covers approximately 2000 years, from the reign of the first king of the 1st Dynasty, Menes, to that of Rameses II. (The period was somewhat too long since no reduction was made when reigns and even whole dynasties overlapped in time.) It also records the enormously long reigns of the gods, including Osiris, Horus and Seth. Between the gods and the time of Menes came two groups of lesser beings, the 'spirits' (see no. 53) and the 'followers of Horus' (see no. 60, 'To follow').

The divide between the reign of the lesser beings and the named kings corresponds with the transition from prehistory to history, through the invention of writing, and with the appearance of a united monarchy. Prior to Menes there would have been no written records of kings and their deeds for the ancient Egyptians to consult.

The primaeval age was a golden age, providing a standard of absolute perfection for the living to match up to. When an expedition in the reign of Queen Hatshepsut reached the land of Punt it was said to be a marvel without equal since the time of 'all these kings who have existed since the primaeval age of the earth'. The qualities of the primaeval age were so taken for granted that the Egyptians did not elaborate on them. Its duration was finite, however. The gods – the primaeval ones – had precise lengths of reign: 7,726 years in the case of Thoth. The Egyptians wrote myths about the gods, such as the quarrel between Horus and Seth, or the attempt by Ra to destroy mankind by unleashing the goddess Hathor against them (see no. 18, 'Beer jug'). These myths were not set in the primaeval age specifically but in a timeless world, and one in which violence occurs.

The Egyptians accepted that the universe had not existed for a past eternity. It had come into existence at a particular moment. They attempted as seriously as they could to visualize the transition from the pre-existence of things to their existence, relying often upon metaphor. One set of images, perhaps the most complicated that the Egyptians developed, involved the creation of life from the primaeval waters (see no. 8, 'Water'). A far simpler image for spontaneous creation used the metaphor of spittle or semen ejected by a creator-god (usually Atum) from which developed not the matter of the universe directly but a hierarchy of gods responsible for various elements of the world (for example, the earth, the sky, and the luminosity of the daytime air). A key figure was the god Khepri, depicted as the scarab beetle, whose name meant 'Becomer' and in whose habits the Egyptians found another metaphor for the inexplicable spontaneous appearance of life (see no. 77, 'To come into existence'). Egyptians saw no need to develop a consistent, standard treatise that pulled together the various different strands of their mythology. They believed that complicated subjects were better covered by parallel explanations of equal validity.

53. SPIRIT

It is not clear if the hieroglyph for spirit – a crested ibis (*Ibis comata*) – was conceptually associated with a bird, or whether it was chosen on account of its phonetic similarity with the bird's name.

In Egyptian life, 'spirits' (the singular is *ȝḫ*, or *akh*) were a distinct category of beings, in one text listed along with people, gods and the dead. In most of the sources 'spirits' are the dead who have been transformed into something radiant, through contact with the sun-god, so that they become minor incarnations of the sun-god themselves. In the New Kingdom, and especially at the necropolis workmen's village of Deir el-Medina, people made small memorial tablets dedicated in each case to a 'perfect spirit (or incarnation) of Ra'. Each tablet had a personal name which is clearly that of a family ancestor; they are our clearest guide to what the word 'spirit' meant. 'Spirits' could be encountered in the Field of Iaru (see no. 15, 'Plough'), where they were each eight cubits (four metres) tall and reaped giant cereals. King

Akhenaten, whose name must mean something like 'incarnation of the Aten', was unique in claiming to be a 'spirit' while still alive: from the Egyptian's point of view this would have been a bold, and even arrogant claim.

In keeping with their view of a primaeval age the Egyptians could not imagine a prehistoric society that was simpler and on a smaller scale than their own, and so they invented a mythical period in which a group of spirits had reigned over Egypt in the distant past, following the era of gods and before the kings (and immediately before an enigmatic group called 'followers of Horus'; see no. 60, 'To follow'). No myths giving names or details about these remote spirits have survived, however.

The adjectival form 'spiritual' meant something like 'glorious', 'beneficial', even 'useful'. To say a person was 'beneficial of heart' was to say that he was compliant and willing to serve. When the word was applied to buildings it probably kept something of its core meaning of divine manifestation. King Tuthmosis III added a large and elaborate stone building at the back of the temple of Amun-Ra at Karnak. One of its functions was to celebrate the king's ancestors, each of whom was represented by a statue. He called the building Akh-menu, which means roughly 'the Most Glorious of Monuments'.

In the uncertain world of the Egyptians, even 'spirits' could change into something threatening. The malevolent forces that entered a house at night seeking to harm the living, in part through bringing sickness, included 'spirits' as well as other ghostly forms. This is another pointer to the fact that outside the world of temples and their confidant portrayals of a universe under control, spiritual forces were fickle; what was supposedly good could suddenly harm, and people had to take the initiative through magic in order to guard themselves (see no. 99, 'Protection').

54. KING

Egypt's line of kings spanned 3000 years, beginning around 3000 BC and ending with Roman emperors, who were depicted on temple walls in all the trappings of their Egyptian precursors even though they belonged to a different culture and rarely, if ever, visited Egypt.

For most of its history ancient Egypt was ruled by hereditary kings who for long periods of time maintained the succession within a single family, or 'dynasty'. The 1st Dynasty won its place through warfare against rival families at a time when Egypt was still in the process of becoming a single united kingdom (see no. 57, 'To unite'). By the time Alexander the Great conquered Egypt in 332 BC, 31 dynasties had ruled. For a long time they were Egyptian. Often we do not know the details of how one dynasty replaced another. The 11th Dynasty, based in the city of Thebes, came to power when the king emerged as the winner in a civil war. The 18th Dynasty, which also came from Thebes, began with the expulsion of the Palestinian Hyksos kings and lasted for nearly 250 years. King Akhenaten was its last major representative. The failure of his unifying religious vision and the early death of his successors (including Tutankhamun) allowed military families from the north of Egypt to take over. For long periods after the end of the 20th Dynasty (around 1000 BC) Egypt was ruled by foreign kings. The Libyan kings of the 22nd Dynasty made Egypt their home, as did, to some extent, the Sudanese (Nubian or Kushite) kings of the 25th Dynasty. To the Persian kings of the 27th Dynasty, however, Egypt was a distant province which they ruled from their homeland of Elam, now an area of Iran close to the border with Iraq.

The power of Egyptian kings rested partly in their claim of divinity and partly in their control of resources. Each king was 'the good god' and his father was the sun-god Ra or, by the New Kingdom, the Theban god Amun-Ra. The king's statues would be found in temples throughout the country, either alongside those of the local god or on their own (see no. 96, 'Statue'). The huge temple at Soleb in Nubia built by Amenhetep III was dedicated solely to a statue of himself. Through a centralized system of administration, kings had access to materials and to labour and were able to build large monuments which glorified themselves and, at the same time, the gods. Some of the largest of the monuments were the kings' own tombs, as in the case of the pyramids of the Old and Middle Kingdoms. Although they did not have a monopoly of armed force (see no. 13, 'Province'), kings could raise larger armies than others. By the New Kingdom the king's army had become a permanent force.

It was the duty of kings to maintain order through just administration and pious deeds for the gods, and to keep Egypt safe from foreign invasion. Kings were expected to be wise as well as to be soldiers who led their armies into battle. They relied upon a circle of advisors and administrators, the principal of whom was the 'vizier' who effectively ran the internal affairs of the country. We have detailed accounts of the elaborate ceremony of the vizier's installation, his duties and the protocol by which his own dignity was maintained. Foremost among his duties was hearing petitions from aggrieved subjects, and adjudicating between conflicting petitions. His audience hall served as the principal law court of Egypt and it was, in theory, open to anyone seeking to present a case. The responsibilities were such that, at the installation of the vizier Rekhmira, the king remarked that being vizier 'is not sweet; it is as bitter as gall. He is the bronze that shields the gold of his master's house.' In the Old Kingdom many viziers, who were also in charge of pyramid building, were sons of kings, but afterwards viziers seem to have been appointed from outside the royal family. This was presumably to limit the threat which such a powerful office posed to the king himself. After the mid-Old Kingdom, princes were generally restricted from adopting a prominent role in society.

This is in contrast to the queens and other women of the king's family – his mother, sisters and daughters. These formed a conspicuous and powerful group given their own palaces, income derived from grants of land, and their own hierarchies of officials. They maintained a staff of female servants and companions. Some of these were daughters of families of the elite, and took the title 'royal ornament', a mark of status which they kept after they married. Some of them were foreigners, brought to Egypt when the king married the daughter of a foreign king. No fewer than 317 of them accompanied Gilukhepa, daughter of the king of Mitanni, when she journeyed to Egypt to marry Amenhetep III. In the reign of Rameses III a group of court women and their male supporters plotted to assassinate the king with the aim of placing a young prince on the throne. The assassination succeeded but not the rest of the plot. Instead the men faced a trial followed either by execution or the honour of suicide. One queen, Hatshepsut, managed to rule Egypt for around 15 years while the prince who had already been chosen as the next king, Tuthmosis III, retired into the background. For a short time after the death of Akhenaten it looks as though his queen, Nefertiti, ruled in her own right.

The majority of kings are no more than names to us. For only a very few can we catch glimpses of individuality, mostly from their reputations. Rameses II was the most successful all-rounder: prolific builder of monumental temples, battle leader and maker of peace with Egypt's great enemy, the kingdom of the Hittites. He fathered at least 100 children whose names and images he included on the walls of his temples. Some 60 years later, Rameses IV prayed: 'You shall double for me the long duration, the great kingship of King Rameses II, the great god' (the prayer failed: he died in his seventh regnal year).

Amenhetep II, another great king, commemorated his physical skills. As an 18-year-old 'he had no equal on the field of battle. He was one who knew horses; there was not his like in this numerous army. Not one among them could draw his bow; he could not be approached in running.' Firing from his chariot, his arrows passed through each of four bronze targets 7.5 centimetres thick.

King Akhenaten introduced a monotheistic version of state religion, based around the worship of the power of the sun, the Aten. Should we count him an intellectual king inspired by a genuine religious vision, or a tyrant who used religion to increase his own power at the expense of the rich and powerful priest-hoods of Egypt, especially that of Amun-Ra of Thebes? The surviving evidence does not tell us. We do not know how large a following his beliefs attracted. After his death his family was ousted by military men from the north and the traditional cults were re-established. He was branded 'that criminal of Akhetaten', and his new city of Tell el-Amarna was abandoned once the court returned to the old capital city of Memphis.

King Khufu, builder of the Great Pyramid, was portrayed in one story as cruel. Having seen a magician reunite the severed head and body of a goose and bring it back to life, Khufu asks for a demonstration on a prisoner. The magician refuses and rebukes the king. Khufu's ill-repute survived for centuries. When the Greek traveller Herodotus visited Egypt 2000 years later, he, too, was told unflattering stories about Khufu.

Statues can help to form our ideas of Egyptians kings. One of Rameses II (in Turin) shows a benign figure that matches his reputation, while statues of kings Senusret III and Amenemhat III of the 12th Dynasty are sometimes glowering, sometimes careworn. These statues either convey an impression of brutal power, or the loneliness and burden of responsibility of supreme office. Some of the predecessors of these kings had expressed the latter sentiment. 'I gave to the beggar, I raised the orphan, I gave success to the poor as to the wealthy. But he who ate my food raised opposition; he to whom I gave my trust used it to plot' are words put into the mouth of the assassinated Amenemhat I in a treatise addressed to his son and heir, King Senusret I. 'Beware of being surrounded by the servants of the enemy. Caution prolongs life,' wrote another king to his son at the time of civil war in the 1st Intermediate Period.

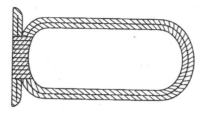

55. CARTOUCHE

The hieroglyph shows a doubled loop of rope, the ends bound tightly around one part of the loop, then spreading out to form a straight line. It is a modification of a sign which shows a circle of rope with the ends unfixed that depicts the concept of a bounded space (thus ○ *šn* or *shen*) and is used as the determinative of the words 'to encircle' and 'circuit' (derived from the same root), referring to the whole world upon which the sun shone. An Egyptian king's aspiration to rule the whole world was said to be over the 'circuit of the sun-disc'. It became a symbol for 'eternity' (the Shen symbol), presumably because the firmly bound loop contained no visible end.

The cartouche version of the sign appeared early in Egyptian history as a frame to pick out the name of the king, written inside the loop. The circular shape had to be elongated to accommodate the necessary line of hieroglyphs. The rope metaphorically contained and controlled the king's territorial realm, perhaps in the way that the wooden beams of a ship were held in place by complex rope lashings (see no. 43, 'Boat travelling upstream').

At their coronation, Egyptian kings were given more than one name. By the beginning of the Middle Kingdom the full set numbered five. The first three, which did not use the cartouche, named the king as a manifestation of the god Horus and of the royal protective cobra and vulture goddesses, Wadjit and Nekhbet, who stood for Lower and Upper Egypt respectively. 'Horus' was the oldest name and had appeared by the time writing began in Egypt just before 3000 BC. A fourth name, written for the first time inside a cartouche, was added at the beginning of the Old Kingdom, and the fifth name, also in a cartouche, appeared intermittently in the later Old Kingdom before becoming obligatory.

The modern practice is to refer to kings by their fifth name (that is, the second of their cartouche names). This was frequently a pious statement about the gods: Amenemhat ('Amun at the forefront'), Djehutymes (or Tuthmosis, 'Thoth has been born'), Amenhetep ('Amun is satisfied'). They sometimes became family traditions. The 12th Dynasty comprised three kings Senusret ('Man of the cobra-goddess') and four kings Amenemhat. The 20th Dynasty produced an unbroken sequence of kings Rameses ('Ra has been born'), in the modern numbering sequence from III to XI. Later came royal families from outside, introducing kings with foreign names: the Libyans Osorkon and Takeloth, the Nubians Taharka and Shabaka, and the Persian Darijava(l)ush, whom the Greeks knew as Darius. Modern Egyptology has failed to find a consensus on spelling many of the kings' names, so that Djehutymes also appears as Thothmes or Tuthmosis, and Amenhetep as Amenophis.

Contemporary texts, however, more often referred to kings by their first cartouche name (the fourth of the full sequence of names). This was composed at the time of coronation, and for a long time was unique to an individual king. First cartouche names make a respectful statement about the sun-god Ra and his spirits (kas): Khakaura ('The kas of Ra have appeared', for Senusret III); Nebmaatra ('The lord of truth is Ra', for Amenhetep III);

Usermaatra ('Powerful of truth is Ra', for Rameses II). The practice of composing a new first cartouche continued with foreign
kings, who kept their own foreign names for their second cartouche. After the Persian King Cambyses had conquered Egypt in
525 BC, a leading Egyptian priest named Udjahor-resenet tells us
that he composed for him his first cartouche, Mesutira ('Offspring
of Ra'), which was in full traditional Egyptian style. The last
known cartouche is a conversion into hieroglyphs of the Latin
name of the Roman Emperor Maximinus Daia, who reigned
between AD 305 and 313 and was one of the last major supporters
of paganism before the Roman Empire became officially
Christian.

The naming process of a new king signalled the start of a new
era throughout the country. All texts, from those to be carved on
temple walls to legal documents and letters on papyrus, would
need immediately to include the new cartouches and the calendar
began again with 'year 1'. In an account of her coronation, the
father of the usurping Queen Hatshepsut is said to have 'commanded that the lector-priests be brought in to proclaim her
official names . . . and to set them on every construction and every
seal (ready) for the coronation.' At the same time it was decreed
that, 'as for anyone who shall hear the name of Her Majesty
spoken, he shall come immediately to tell the king'. This cannot
mean that people were forbidden from mentioning the name of
the reigning king. Rameses II, for example, was known to his subjects familiarly as Sesi. Most likely it refers to disrespectful or even
treasonable mentions. This created, of course, an opportunity for
maliciousness. The chief workman of Deir el-Medina, named
Hay, was accused by some of his workers of uttering a curse
against the reigning king, Seti II. He brought it before an unofficial
court at which point the men withdrew the accusation, receiving
'100 severe blows of the stick' each, for trying to cause trouble.

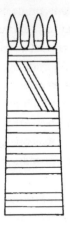

56. PALACE

The hieroglyph shows a building of matting on wooden frames, with a row of loose plant fronds along the top. It writes the standard word for 'palace'. The sign derives from a time before the 1st Dynasty when, either in reality or in the imagination of Egyptians of later times (see no. 10, 'Papyrus column'), palaces were built with these materials. In dynastic times, palaces were normally built from the same perishable sun-dried mud-bricks as were the houses of Pharaohs' subjects. They were not monuments built for eternity and few examples have survived, most from the New Kingdom. At any one time there were probably a host of them scattered across the country, providing accommodation for the king throughout his realm. They ranged from single buildings – like grander versions of the houses of high officials – to sprawling complexes, the best known example being the palace-town of King Amenhetep III at Malkata, western Thebes, which covered an area of at least 16 hectares (see no. 95, 'Festival').

Palaces had to be designed to proclaim the dignity of kingship and to safeguard it from dangers by setting up barriers, most simply through progressions of halls of columns leading to a throne room. Another way of maintaining a distance between the king and his subjects was through the use of a 'window of appearance' (see no. 7, 'To appear'), through which the king would hand down rewards to chosen followers. Palaces had distinctive internal decoration which set them apart from even the houses of the very rich and powerful. Walls, ceilings and sometimes the floors of palaces were brightly painted, often with scenes from nature, which must have helped to relieve the formality of life at court.

Contemporaries wrote in praise that the new palace of Rameses II in the delta was 'radiant with halls of lapis lazuli and turquoise'. Although precious stones might have been used, much of the effect was created by means of glazed tiles. Sections of an elaborate throne dais made from turquoise-coloured tiles have been found on the site. The glazed treads of the palace's steps were decorated with figures of Egypt's enemies, and the balustrades ended with statues of lions in the act of devouring foreign captives. Sinuhe, a returned exile forgiven for an assumed act of treachery, describes being called back for a royal audience:

> When it dawned, very early, they came to summon me. Ten men came and ten men went to usher me into the palace. My forehead touched the ground between the sphinxes, and the royal children stood in the gateway to meet me. The courtiers who usher through the forecourt set me on the way to the audience hall. I found his majesty on the great throne in a kiosk of gold. Stretched out on my belly, I did not know myself before him, while this god greeted me pleasantly. I was like a man seized by darkness.

All ends well. The princesses are brought in and sing a hymn of praise to the king, their father, and work into it a plea for forgiveness. The king obliges and gives Sinuhe a place at court, with a pension. 'I left the audience hall, the princesses giving me their hands.'

Palaces were the centre of government. The king ruled with the help of his senior officials, including his vizier. After discussing matters he would make pronouncements and issue decrees, copies of which, if they were on subjects of wide application, would be sent by messengers throughout the country. Some of these pronouncements were 'laws', but they were not necessarily remembered by the name of the king who made them. When a case came to be judged, it was enough to declare: 'The Law of Pharaoh states . . .' Part of the business of state was maintaining correspondence with foreign rulers, some of them heads of powerful independent kingdoms and others clients of the Pharaoh in the Egyptian empire. Those in the Near East corresponded in a Semitic language written in cuneiform script impressed into mud tablets. Among the Pharaoh's staff were translators who had to tell him what the letters said, and then compose his replies. A hoard of more than 300 of these letters (the Amarna Letters) was discovered buried beneath the floor of an office at Akhenaten's city of Tell el-Amarna.

In addition to officials with specific jobs were courtiers whose high rank kept them close to the king and who acted as his companions and advisors. They bore titles like 'fan-bearer on the right hand of the king' and 'cup-bearer'. A man's chances of royal favour must have been helped if he was a good hunter, since many scenes record the king hunting game in the desert accompanied by his court. (Before the New Kingdom the huntsmen, including the king, were on foot; subsequently they hunted in chariots.) Such men did not necessarily live in the palace grounds, however. At Akhenaten's city of Tell el-Amarna, where the evidence is better preserved than elsewhere, many courtiers and high officials, including the vizier, lived in houses among the suburbs up to two kilometres from the nearest palace, making journeys into the centre of the city to meet the king.

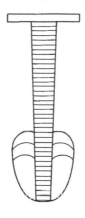

57. TO UNITE

The hieroglyph shows lungs and a windpipe (not to be confused with the *nfr* sign, see no. 24, 'Good'), the word for which had the same series of sounds – *s* + *m* + *ȝ* = *smȝ* (*sema*) – as the verb 'to unite'.

The greatest periods of stability and prosperity in Egyptian history arose when the country was ruled by one king at the head of a single administration. These periods we know as the Old, Middle and New Kingdoms. During the other 'intermediate' periods, Egypt was divided into several independent or semi-independent territories ruled by men who might claim the title of king or accept a lesser title. During the last centuries of ancient Egyptian history, the Late Period, when Egypt was for long periods ruled by foreign kings, the contrast between unity and disunity was less obvious.

The king had a duty to 'unite' the country against fragmentation and the local fighting that would inevitably follow. His coronation involved a ceremony of symbolic re-unification. Modern reconstructions of the formation of the first ancient Egyptian state see the process of unification as a complex interplay among several ambitious families of local rulers. In their mythology, however, the Egyptians imagined that their country had originally been home to only two separate kingdoms, the north and the south, each under the patronage of a separate god (Horus and Seth). Each had its own symbols, including distinctive crowns, creatures (the vulture for the south, the cobra for the north) and plants (papyrus for the north and either a type of reed or the lotus for the south). Combining or juxtaposing them expressed political unity. On the forehead of King Tutankhamun's gold mask, for example, the heads of vulture and cobra sit side by side; in carved and painted scenes the plants grow intertwined, their stems tied together in a knot around the vertical shaft of the 'unity' sign.

On their accession, kings were given special names (see no. 55, 'Cartouche), and some of these reflected the king's role as the bringer of unity. Teti was known as 'who placates the two lands', Pepi I as 'who loves the two lands', Sankhkara Menthuhetep as 'who brings to life the two lands', Amenemhat I as 'who pleases the two lands', and Nebhepetra Menthuhetep and the Persian King Cambyses as 'who unites the two lands'. The full name of the new administrative capital built near Memphis by King Amenemhat I after a period of instability was 'Amenemhat seizes the two lands' (Amenemhat-ith-tawy, often abbreviated by the Egyptians to Ith-tawy).

58. TRUTH (MAAT)

The Egyptians believed that invisibly present behind the experience of living there lay a guiding force that tipped the balance
towards order, harmony, truth and justice. This they called 'Maat',
m3ʕt, and in it they summed up civilized values as they saw them.
To write the word a single ostrich feather is used as the hieroglyph. It vividly expresses weightlessness, but we do not know if
this is the full explanation.

The goddess Maat, 𓏏𓄿𓆄, was the daughter of the sun-god
Ra, who had come from the primaeval mound, the place of creation, only 'after he had set Maat in the place of chaos'. Kings
inherited the responsibility for ensuring that she remained there.
In the prophecy of the priest Neferti a period of chaos and con-
fusion is ended by the coming of a good king when 'Maat will
come into her place while disorder is driven out'. In temple ritual
the king made a symbolic presentation of an image of Maat to the
gods. Some kings incorporated Maat into their names. Thus

Sneferu was 'lord of Maat', and Amenhetep III was 'the lord of Maat is Ra'. In a story from a private library at Deir el-Medina the opposition between Maat and disorder becomes a more obviously moral tale for ordinary people. Based on the myth of the conflict between Horus and Seth, the tale concerns two brothers called Truth and Falsehood. Truth's fate is to be blinded and work as Falsehood's door-keeper, although after a series of fantastic episodes the roles are reversed and it is Falsehood who becomes Truth's blind door-keeper, aided by his loyal but vengeful son.

Kings and the sun-god were said to 'live on Maat' as if it were their food; one text made the contrast with the Nile god Haapy who lived on fish. The king who promoted this idea most strongly was Akhenaten who constantly referred to himself as 'living on truth (Maat)'. His main interest was in revealing what lay at the heart of theology when this was stripped of its endless irrelevant additions (as he saw it) of gods and myths. To him, therefore, Maat perhaps meant 'religious truth'.

Maat, like our term 'justice', was dispensed by the ministers of the king. At the installation of the vizier Rekhmira, his king (Tuthmosis III) addresses him: 'My Majesty knows that decisions are many and there is no end to them, and the judgement of cases never flags. May you act according as I say. Then will Maat rest in her place.' Afterwards Rekhmira acknowledges his responsibility by calling himself 'priest of Maat', a figurative term rather than meaning that he had priestly duties in a temple of Maat.

Egyptians believed in an ultimate judgement after death, based on the conduct of their lives. When a person was led into the hall of Osiris on their death, their 'truth' would be measured on a scale (see no. 90, 'Balance'). Their heart would be balanced against a feather, the symbol of Maat, which also expressed lightness. The god Thoth stood ready to record the result, and the god Anubis checked to see that the balance was properly set up. If the balance did not tilt, a person was considered 'true of voice' and allowed to enter the kingdom of Osiris. A creature which combined the head of a crocodile, foreparts of a lion and hindquarters of a hippopotamus and whose name meant 'Eater of the Dead' stood waiting, in case the balance did tilt. The phrase 'true of voice' was found as an epitaph on memorial stones and tombs, immediately following the name of the deceased, in expectation that the owner had satisfactorily passed the test.

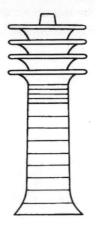

59. TO BE STABLE

The details of the hieroglyph do not allow us to judge exactly what it represents. It is a pillar with a layered top, and one interpretation is that it shows a single tree trunk with the remains of lopped-off branches. It writes the word 'stability', *ḏdt* (*djedet*) and is itself the Djed-pillar, the design for a common amulet.

'Stability' was a key ingredient in an ordered world, and a potent power in itself. It was, together with 'life' and 'dominion', a quality which the gods gave to the reigning king. The pillar of the hieroglyph gained its power when ritually set upright. Temple scenes show a ceremony in which a large pillar of this shape was raised vertically from a leaning position by the king, in the presence of the gods. Such an act, of moving from potential to completion, also signified rebirth. The ritual was performed for deceased kings, and the distinctive shape of the pillar was turned into an amulet to accompany the dead generally, so that all could benefit. A link was made with Osiris by attaching to the pillar some of his characteristics: it was given a pair of arms holding the crook and flail, and the distinctive crown of Osiris made from two ostrich feathers side by side above a pair of long curly ram's horns. Egyptians took delight in enriching symbols by adding further elements.

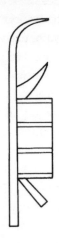

60. TO FOLLOW

The hieroglyph shows a knife and another object tied to a staff with a curving top. The details and significance are obscure, though the temptation is to see it as an equivalent of the bundled axe and rods, the emblem of authority carried before Roman magistrates. The sign writes the word ꜽ𓏭𓈖 *šms* (shemes), 'to follow' and 𓋴𓏭𓈖 *šmsw* (shemsu), 'follower' in contexts which are frequently mundane, as in a man's description of his old age: 'My legs refuse to follow.' In connection with gods and kings, however, the sign and the word take on a special significance.

The hieroglyph appears in representations of the Otherworld as a free-standing symbol, with the knife emphasized. Sometimes it stands in the barque of the sun-god. At other times the severed heads of some of the demons of the Otherworld are suspended from it. From this we might conclude that the sign symbolizes the potential retribution that accompanies the possession of absolute power.

The sign is closely associated with the kingship of early Egypt. During the first two dynasties the king and his entourage made a journey every other year to inspect his country and to remind everyone where their loyalty lay. Each king was an embodiment of the falcon-god Horus, and even directly referred to as Horus. The brief historical records for this time call these journeys the 'following of Horus' (or 'progress of Horus') and add a picture of a boat. Perhaps it was on these occasions that the king's retainers and bodyguards carried the bundles of objects represented in the hieroglyph as symbols of his authority and power to punish. The term for those who accompanied him, his 'followers', had legendary status. The 'followers of Horus' (the archetypal king), were, together with spirits (see no. 53), listed as rulers of Egypt during the transitional period between the reigns of the gods and the first historical kings of the early dynasties. Whereas the word 'spirit' was generally benign, 'follower' in this context perhaps echoed the local warfare which had preceded the final unification of Egypt.

Much knowledge that the Egyptians took for granted is largely lost to us because they did not consider it necessary to write it down. Time and again we are left guessing at the layers of meaning which Egyptians attached to individual objects which, on their own, convey little.

61. ENEMY

The Egyptians defined themselves not just through geography and culture but through contrast with their enemies. Regarded as inferiors, these enemies were any people that lay outside Egypt's boundaries, but close enough to pose a threat. Their predisposition to menace Egypt provided a justification for the Pharaoh to attack them. One common word for enemies means literally 'one already laid low, fallen', 𓆓𓃀𓏏 ḥrw (*kheru*), and takes as its determinative a picture of a prostrate man bleeding profusely from a head wound. The word is often combined with the adjective for 'vile', 'cowardly' or 'base', 𓄣𓏏 ḥsỉ (*khesi*), which takes the sparrow determinative. Pictures or statues of defeated enemies, kneeling dejectedly with their arms fastened behind them by a rope at the elbows, sometimes simultaneously being savaged by a lion, were stock elements in the repertoire of court artists. Rows of these figures, roped together and amounting to several hundred, each one accompanied by a place name, helped to underline the king's supremacy over the known world in scenes, often on temple walls, that show him in the pose of conqueror.

Between 3000 and 1500 BC Egypt's enemies were either weakly organized tribal societies in Nubia and the surrounding deserts, or minor states in Palestine. The Egyptians saw them as serious threats only because over this long period of time they themselves had not yet elevated warfare and militarism to be a major feature of their society (see no. 85, 'Soldier'). This only began to develop during the New Kingdom, but even then the Egyptian empire remained fairly modest in scope. Egyptian armies were regularly checked by those of medium-sized states on the borders of Syria, primarily the kingdoms of Mitanni and of the Hittites. The Egyptians never developed their military on the scale of the Assyrians, Persians and Romans, who were able to subjugate distant major kingdoms, Egypt included.

Egyptian contempt for their enemies was more cultural than ethnic, and when large numbers of prisoners of war and sometimes aristocratic hostages were brought into the country, in time they were integrated into the population of Egypt, there being no concept of citizenship. Indeed, the Egyptians had a long tradition of employing foreign soldiers, some of whom settled in Egypt permanently. The Egyptian population was, in actuality, of diverse origin, and what made people Egyptian was adherence to the norms of Egyptian culture.

Fear and hatred were directed towards anyone who might pose a threat to stability. Particularly during the Middle Kingdom, scribes wrote lists of the enemies of the state on pottery vessels or on figurines of bound captives, which we term Execration Texts. After reading out a curse the figurines were probably symbolically knifed or, in the case of the pottery vessels, deliberately smashed. When excavating one place where the ceremony was performed, outside an Egyptian fortress in Nubia named Mirgissa, archaeologists found the bones of a man who had probably been beheaded at the time along with many examples of the Execration Texts. Presumably he was a captured Nubian. Mostly the lists on Execration Texts are of foreign princes and their people, but they also included as a general category 'all the Egyptians who are with them', and even individually named Egyptians who had presumably planned treason. One of these, Intefiker, a son of the like-named vizier, was stated to be already dead, but he remained nonetheless a threatening spirit. Some of these texts were buried in Egyptian cemeteries.

The parallel universe of the Otherworld and the journey of the sun-god with whom the deceased king merged were likewise perpetually under threat from enemies called 'the gang of Seth'. They personified the forces of disturbance, and existed to be cast down and to receive punishment. They walked upside down, ate their own excrement, were dismembered and defleshed; their shadows were destroyed. They were assigned to an 'outer darkness' and to a 'slaughtering place' where they were punished in fiery pits and cauldrons by demons who were some of the dead.

In real life, enemies of the king or those who transgressed against the gods also faced harsh punishments: death by impalement, or burning (though the high-born conspirators who plotted against Rameses III were allowed to take their own lives).

62. BOW

The use of the bow extends back to the Stone Age. In a cemetery at Gebel Sahaba beside the Nile in northern Sudan, dating to around 10,000 BC, many of the dead had been pierced by flint arrowheads. For a long time Egyptians used a 'simple' longbow, usually between 1.3 and 1.7 metres long, made from various types of wood, including acacia, and bent to shape by holding it under tension in steam for some time. Early in the New Kingdom, however, as part of the radical change in weapons and tactics, when Egyptians adopted the practices of their enemies in the Near East, they began to manufacture shorter but more powerful composite bows made from a core of wood with a layer of sinew on the back and horn on the front. Without its string and no longer under tension, it fitted into a long triangular box, often decorated, which became a conspicuous accessory on the side of chariots. The youthful Amenhetep II would have used a bow of this kind to pierce a bronze target with his arrows (see no. 7 'To appear' and no. 54, 'King').

The bow, an image of war, became a symbol of the king's enemies, collectively known as the 'Nine Bows', though why nine was significant is not known. The Egyptians created a design in which groups of three of these bows alternated with pictures of ethnically differentiated foreign captives, then drew it where the king would set his feet, such as in areas of painted flooring in the palace that led to the throne, on his footstool, even on the soles of his sandals. Thus the king would constantly trample on his enemies. Nubia, a stretch of the Nile valley that extended southwards from Aswan and the ancient Egyptian frontier, was particularly identified with the bow and known as 'the land of the bow', 𓈉 *T3-Sty* (*Ta-sety*), using an archaic word for 'bow'. Its inhabitants were 'the bowlanders'. The Egyptians in time turned this to their advantage, so that 'the bowmen of Kush' (another term for Nubia) took their place in the Egyptian army.

63. MAN AND WOMAN

Most of what we know about ancient Egypt derives from a tiny minority of affluent men. These were the literate officials who were often landowners as well. A few of them, who gained lasting reputations (such as Ptahhetep), recorded their views on life in manuals of good conduct written for their sons and fellow men. They pay little attention to women. When they do, they can be generous towards them.

Good speech is more hidden than greenstone, yet may be found amongst maids at the grindstone.

But more often patronizing at the same time.

Do not control your wife in her house when you know she is efficient. Do not say to her 'Where is it? Get it!' when she has put it in the right place. Let your eye observe in silence, then you will recognize her qualities. It is a joy when your hand is with her.

Fill her belly, clothe her back. Ointment soothes her body.
Gladden her heart as long as you live. She is a fertile field for
her lord.

A more direct expression of misogyny is found in the short
and cynical precepts of Ankhsheshonk (though several centuries
later than the other sources). To him women are grasping, unre-
liable and stupid: 'Instructing a woman is like having a sack of
sand whose side is split open.' We have so few records made by
women that it is not possible to build up an independent picture of
how they viewed their role or their men.

We can infer how men and women behaved towards one
another by studying individual instances. Relations were the outcome of constant negotiation within a social system that gave to
men the greater share of overt authority but did not prescribe a
particular place to women. Men obliged to be away from home
might leave their wives to run the household. The priestess
Henut-tawy wrote to her husband, with a frankness that suggests
mutual confidence, to record how, when she checked a consign-
ment of grain, she found several sacks missing. On hearing the
men's excuse, she took it as a prelude to further disasters: 'I kept
my silence at that moment, saying, "By the time you return the
god Amun will have done every bad thing with me."' Some
women, perhaps through widowhood, found themselves officially
recognized as renters of temple farmland – a common alternative
to outright land ownership – alongside various ranks of men.

One role for women was of priestess, which gained in status as
time passed, particularly during and after the New Kingdom.
Many bore the title 'songstress' or 'chantress' of a god. Pictures
show them as part of a group, their body positions suggestive of
dancing. Whether they sang in words (none are recorded) or ulu-
lated we do not know. Some of them came from wealthy families
and were buried in elaborately decorated coffins accompanied by
finely painted copies of the Book of the Dead. Between 870 and
525 BC, among the most prominent people at Thebes, there was a
line of 'god's wives of Amun', although how much temporal

power they wielded is hard to know. They lived in a palace attached to the temple at Medinet Habu originally built to commemorate Rameses III, and were buried in vaults beneath small mortuary temples of their own which lay alongside. Each one was the daughter of a king, seems not to have married, and passed the office on to her successor through a process of adoption.

The clearest picture of women's lives that we have comes from the abundant sources that survive from the workmen's village of Deir el-Medina and the adjacent town of western Thebes, written during the later New Kingdom. Women wrote short letters to one another, revealing that some of them at least were literate, though we do not know whether they learned at home or were allowed into the scribal schools. Often they addressed each other as 'sister' but this was an expression of affection: 'Said by Isis to [her] sister Nebu-emnu: I implore you to weave for me this shawl, very, very quickly, before Amenhetep [the local patron god] comes, because I am completely naked.' Women haggled with passing (male) traders to buy slave girls, they raised crops to sell at market, they joined their menfolk in conspiracy and theft. They appeared in court, though far less frequently than men, accused of theft, non-payment, selling a building improperly, and neglecting a sick relative. When faced with proof that the lady Herya had stolen and buried a bronze chisel and a piece of bronze sacred image, the court declared her worthy of death, and handed her over to the jurisdiction of the vizier (with what result we do not know). Outside the probably all-male scribal offices women and men seem to have shared a wide range of experiences. Theirs was not a segregated society.

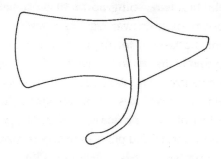

64. RAZOR

Apart from a time in the Old Kingdom when small moustaches came into fashion, during none of the historic periods did men retain facial hair. Full beards were one sign of being foreign. Thus shaving must have been a regular feature of daily life for men. Many examples have been found of implements of the shape of the hieroglyphic determinative for 'razor', the flat blade of copper or bronze attached to a curving handle, often of wood.

The actual bodies of ancient Egyptians, when sufficiently well preserved, show that men cropped their hair fairly close and sometimes completely shaved the scalp, but that women often grew their hair long. Both men and women could change their appearance by using artificial hair additions. They could thicken or lengthen their hair by tying in extra pieces, as did an 11th Dynasty soldier from a mass grave who had thickened his hair with tightly wound additional spirals, or Queen Tetisheri, whose thinning white hair had been supplemented with more substantial braids of brown.

To enhance their status, however, and give the impression of having longer hair elaborately prepared, Egyptians preferred wigs. The foundation was a netting cap usually made of hair itself. Woven into it were plaits, with braids or curls, depending on the preferred style, braids reaching up to 50 centimetres in length. Warmed beeswax or resin was used as a setting agent. By the New Kingdom the fashion for men was a two-layered wig, the lower of long thin plaits (up to several hundred of them) and the upper of open-centre curls. When not worn wigs were kept in boxes. Women's wigs were less elaborate and so appeared more naturalistic. Most of our information on the Egyptians' appearance comes from statues and pictures from their tombs, in which they show themselves to best advantage. We have no way of knowing for how much of a day people would actually wear the larger wigs.

For male priests on duty in the temple, hair was a sign of impurity, even though the gods themselves were often shown wearing heavy wigs. The statement by Herodotus that Egyptian priests shaved their bodies all over is at least partly borne out by the many depictions of priests, especially in later periods, with shaven heads, although this was not as important as purification through washing and the use of natron (see no. 3, 'Grain'). That the large temple of Amun at Thebes maintained on its staff a 'chief of barbers of Amun' implies the presence of a whole team to make sure that the priests kept to the required standard of cleanliness. The association of hair with ritual uncleanliness seems not to have applied to priestesses, however.

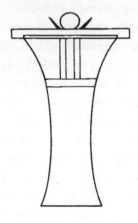

65. UNGUENT

Oils and unguents were so valuable they were usually transported and stored in small and often distinctive containers. The hieroglyph shows a slightly flaring tubular stone jar, its flat lid secured with string. According to present evidence the Egyptians did not practise distillation and could not make perfumes, which are distilled from scented parts of plants. Instead they steeped fragrant plant substances in oil or fat, either by cold pressing or by boiling, to create scented unguents or ointments. We know that the wood and resin of various trees not native to Egypt, including cedar from Lebanon, were some of the ingredients used. They would have given off a warm, rich, tangy aroma.

Unguents were smeared over the body, of both women and men: 'I wish I were her laundryman . . . I would wash away the unguent from her clothes and wipe my body with her dress,' opines a love-sick man. It came in jars, and an elegant way of dispensing it was to scoop out a little with a delicately carved spoon into which, one supposes, the fingers were dipped. In the many scenes of banqueting in Egyptian tombs of the New Kingdom, the women wear a cone-shaped object on the crown of their heads and, in some, brown streaks descend over their fine linen shawls: a common interpretation is that the cones are of viscous unguent which, over the course of a warm evening, slowly melted, re-anointing the skin and giving off its scent as it did so.

Seven jars of unguent were buried with the dead, each containing a different variety of oil or unguent. Ancient Egyptian texts do not tell us the ingredients, however, although the name of one does derive from that of a fragrant tree that might be cedar. The formulae for unguents might have been quite complicated because 'medical' texts, which contain recipes for curative compounds, show that the Egyptians maintained a tradition of mixing unusual ingredients.

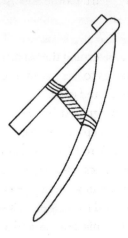

66. TO LOVE

The word 'to love', written mrỉ (meri), is depicted through the sign of the common wooden hoe, similar in its sound but un-related to the concept of love. The term covered as wide a spectrum of feelings as its English counterpart. Gods loved the king and truth, parents loved children. A person loved life (while hating death), and there were places that the soul loved (or desired). The New Kingdom has left us several collections of songs or poems on the theme of romantic love, and in these the word clearly conveys passion:

> I am held fast by my love; alone, my heart meets your heart;
> from your beauty I'll not part.

> Let not the people say of me 'A woman laid low by love!'

Romantic, sexual love, celebrated even when painful, surfaces only in these poetic texts.

An hour out of eternity flowed to me, while I slept with you.
You have uplifted my heart. Come sorrow, come joy, be not
ever far from me.

Otherwise the sources concerning the relations between men and
women confine themselves to the pragmatic aspects of marriage
and to instances of sexual predation.

Marriage was not recognized by the Egyptian theological
system, which steadfastly kept away from the detailed affairs of
humans and provided no sacred book of guidance. Even the manuals of instruction on ethics and behaviour, one of the most
popular forms of literature in ancient Egypt, gave the topic only
passing comment compared to their extensive advice on the relations between a man and his seniors and juniors: 'Take a wife
while you are young, that she make a son for you. She should bear
for you while you are youthful. It is proper to procreate. Happy
the man whose progeny are many.'

The king maintained a harim, but this seems not to have been
copied even by rich officials. The references to marriage that we
do have imply that a man had one wife to whom, as 'mistress of
the house', he delegated authority within his household. He could
take in other women as sexual partners, texts distinguishing
between wives and women who are 'with' a man, but they were
not given a status of their own, as in the case of the royal harim.
Nor is it clear if women occupied a separate, more secluded part
of the house. A rare glimpse of family life comes from the letters
of the farmer Hekanakht, writing home during an absence. He
had recently remarried, probably after the death of his first wife,
and in response to his family's disapproval of his choice, he writes:
'Would one of you be patient when his wife was denounced to
him? In what way can I be at the same table with you? Shall you
not respect my new wife?' As a solution (and presumably for both
his and her comfort) he asks that she be sent from home to him.

We know next to nothing about how people chose partners or
had them chosen, or about marriage ceremonies. In the love songs
of the New Kingdom the pining lovers often seem to be relative

strangers to one another, but this was not necessarily typical for Egyptian society. A touching case, which illustrates how complex marital relationships could be, is that of a childless widow, Ninefer. Her slave girl had three children (presumably fathered by the widow's deceased husband), all of whom had behaved well towards her. In recognition she allowed her younger brother to marry one of the girls, gave all three of them their freedom and, along with the brother, made them heirs to her property.

Men and women came to marriage with property of their own (sometimes no more than a few household goods) and retained ownership of their belongings. It was also proper for the man to give extra property to his intended wife. In one case of second marriage the husband had to get the agreement of his existing children to give four slaves to his bride, the lady Anoksunedjem. No less a person than the vizier himself comments upon the case, emphasizing that a man's obligations to the woman he lived with outweighed all others: 'Even if it had not been his wife but a Syrian or Nubian whom he loved and to whom he gave property of his, who should counter what he did?'

Along with marriage came infidelity. The teachings of the sage Ptahhetep offer pious advice against casual liaisons: 'If you want to maintain friendship in the house you enter as master, brother, or friend, wherever you enter, beware of approaching the women! . . . A short moment like a dream, then death comes from having known them.' Blame could fall on either or both parties. In a tale of magicians, a priest named Webaoner takes his revenge upon a man who is seeing too much of his wife. He makes a wax crocodile which comes to life and seizes him. He burns the guilty wife in a field, her ashes being cast into the river.

No legal codes have survived from ancient Egypt, so we cannot say whether rape and seduction contravened a particular law. What is clear is that they caused offence in the community and were seen as evidence of undesirable conduct, along with thefts, beatings and acts of impiety. There came a point when offensive behaviour could no longer be tolerated. A list of a person's offences would be presented to a higher official, to secure a trial on the grounds of persistent misconduct. That the law itself might have been neutral in the face of sexual misconduct on its own is suggested by a case in which a servant, finding a skilled workman in bed with his bride-to-be, complained to the magistrates who ordered him (and not the skilled workman, his superior) to be given 100 blows, with the warning words, 'Now, what did you say?'

67. SISTRUM

The sistrum was a religious musical instrument, used by women in the cult of the goddess Hathor and other goddesses. Akhenaten's daughters used it in their adoration of the sun, the Aten. It had no place in secular music performances, such as those staged at banquets. Except for the handle, it was made from metal. When it was picked up and shaken by the handle back and forth, the metal rods would slide from side to side, producing a tinkling sound. The top of the handle was decorated with a face of the goddess Hathor, and in more elaborate designs her face was crowned with a box in the shape of a shrine or temple. This version inspired a distinctive type of architectural column found in Hathor temples (the best-known example being at Dendera in Upper Egypt, 50 kilometres north of Luxor), which resembles the handle of a sistrum with its ornamental top.

Hathor was most widely worshipped as a kindly protective goddess. Although temples were built in her honour, Egyptians detected her presence in natural places, in the rustling leaves of the sycomore tree (see no. 12, 'Tree') and in places in the desert, especially where there was a conspicuous outcrop of rock. Shrines were built to her at mining camps and garrison forts, the largest of them being at the turquoise mines in the southern mountainous part of Sinai, where she was worshipped as 'Hathor Lady of Turquoise'. Egyptian traders and mariners reaching the port of Byblos on the Lebanese coast could celebrate their safe passage at a local shrine of 'Hathor Lady of Byblos'.

Hathor had the power to see a person's destiny. In a story about a doomed prince, as soon as the previously barren queen gives birth to her son, a group of Hathor goddesses visit him to foretell his fate, concluding that: 'He will die through the snake, or the crocodile or the dog.' Whether this happens we do not know for the end of the story is lost. The king's first step was to have him shut away in a remote though luxurious palace for safekeeping.

The discovery of wooden penis models at Hathor's shrine at western Thebes is testimony to her role as a patroness of procreation and childbirth. As the 'goddess of love, of singing, of dance, and the sistrum' she was equated with a release and freedom similar to goddesses in other societies. She made drunkenness from beer acceptable (see no. 18, 'Beer jug'). The Greeks equated her with Aphrodite.

Her cult was not exclusively female. Men as well as women recorded their piety at Hathor shrines, mostly on small stone memorial stelae, and, at her shrine at western Thebes, in pictures painted on linen tunics which had been left behind. What made the cult of Hathor special was that it emphasized a worship of feminine values in a society that normally gave priority to men.

Egyptian pictures on temple walls and on commemorative stelae portrayed her cult as dignified, but the tinkling sound of the shaken sistrum is likely to have encouraged Egyptians who associated her with beer drinking and procreation to abandon the restraint that was so urged upon them by the manuals of ethical instruction.

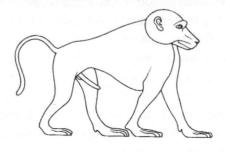

68. BABOON

In Egyptian mythology and tales, animals were sometimes imbued with human characteristics or made the object of human comparison. In the Tale of Two Brothers (c. 1200 BC) the younger brother is warned by talking cows that his vengeful elder brother is waiting behind the door to kill him. This tendency had a humorous side. A few papyri and scribal practice pieces on flakes of limestone from the New Kingdom take standard scenes from tombs and temples and, in wordless storybook form, replace the human figures with animals, rather like modern cartoons. A mouse Pharaoh in a chariot attacks a fortress defended by cat soldiers, while a troupe of musicians is made up of a donkey, lion, crocodile and monkey.

It was in baboons that the Egyptians found the closest parallel to human behaviour. Baboons were not native to Egypt, but a tame population was maintained through importation. Pictures show them brought to the Pharaoh's court as a tribute by foreign peoples of the southern region. They appear in tomb pictures assisting men picking figs, or held on leads by men in scenes of village markets, as if they were policing them. In one case a baboon grabs a running man – is he a thief? – by the leg. Statuettes of baboons (and monkeys, too) depicted them performing human activities: playing musical instruments, grooming hair, practising acrobatics and driving a chariot.

Baboons were not just play creatures to be satirized; they also, paradoxically, were representatives of the god of wisdom and language, Thoth. Scribes venerated Thoth as a baboon, and in the last centuries of Egyptian culture, when the cult of animals became widespread, sacred baboons became oracles. How they delivered their answers to the questions put to them by priests is not recorded. Perhaps the skill of the priests lay in their ability to interpret the baboon's caperings and chatterings.

69. TO HEAR

The hieroglyph depicts the ear either of a cow or a donkey, and is the determinative for the verb 'to hear', 𓂋𓄿 *sḏm* (*sedjem*), as well as for the word for a human ear. A word for a servant is one who 'hears the voice' (of his master). The choice of an animal rather than a human ear is an example of the idiosyncratic nature of hieroglyphic script and it did not trouble the Egyptians, even when the words applied to the gods: 'Amun, lend your ear to the lonely in court. He is poor; he is not rich,' says one prayer included in a scribe's practice book. Statues of gods and kings in temples, and even the heavy stone frames of temple gateways, had the capacity to 'hear prayers'. A way to encourage this was simply to carve one or more ears on a little stone tablet, perhaps adding the name of the god and one's own name, and leaving it with the priests. In these cases, however, the ears are human. One man paid for a statue of himself holding a model of the battlemented wall of the temple of Ptah at Memphis with a human ear carved at the top of each of its towers.

When imagining the sounds that the ancient Egyptians would have heard, we must forget machine and traffic noise, and the low background hum that accompanies modern life. Sounds of nature predominated, from areas of vegetation largely untouched by human development – thickets of trees and marshland supporting a diversity and abundance of birds whose noise filled the air, especially at sunrise and sunset. The human population was, by modern standards, very small, rising from around one million in the 1st Dynasty to perhaps three million at the time of the Roman conquest. The towns were not much more than villages, places of narrow streets and sound-absorbing mud-brick walls. Donkeys brayed by day and dogs, sometimes in semi-wild packs, barked at night.

Crowds of people were rarely large. Sometimes their noise was that of celebration and release, with perhaps the banging of tambourines and drums. Sometimes there was the wail of mourning women at the time of a funeral. Occasionally there was the cry of protest. Records have survived of demonstrations at western Thebes by state workmen who, when their ration payments failed to appear, stopped work and marched to the nearest temples that housed their supplies, but fewer than 100 people are likely to have been involved. Other records from the same place document domestic disputes which might have brought the whole village of around 70 families out into the streets, which were so narrow that few people could walk along them side by side. The loudest of human sounds, the roar and cries of armed men clashing, came only during the short periods of civil war and when foreign armies invaded during the last centuries of Egyptian history.

Despite the relative quiet of their lives, the Egyptians still distinguished 'silence' with a word of its own. Silence was a characteristic of cemeteries in the desert, known as 'the land which loves silence'. The desert cliffs of western Thebes shielded an area of steep-sided valleys where, in the New Kingdom, kings were buried in decorated chambers reached by long corridors cut into the rock, the whole of which is called in modern times the Valley of Kings. It was presided over by a cobra-goddess whose name was simply 'She who loves silence'. Egyptian books of instruction in good conduct express an admiration for the man with an economy of words, the 'silent man'. Through silence came an inner strength and authority.

70. MOUTH

In contrast to the sign for 'ear', the Egyptian hieroglyph for 'mouth' is the human mouth, and serves commonly to write the words for 'utterance', 'speech' and 'language'. The speaking of Egyptian language was the clearest mark of Egyptianness. In Palestine, the exiled fugitive courtier Sinuhe was comforted by the prince who befriends him with the words, 'You will be happy with me; you will hear the speech of Egypt.' That sound is, however, lost to us now. The hieroglyphic script wrote mainly consonants and strongly emphasized vowels and does not reveal enough information for a working reconstruction of the sounds of the language. A handful of Egyptian words turn up in the cuneiform script of the ancient Near East (in the Amarna Letters; see no. 56, 'Palace'), which acts as a guide to pronunciation. These words hint at how wide the gap had become between ancient Egyptian spelling and speech. For example, the name of the eldest daughter of King Akhenaten is written in hieroglyphs as if it were

pronounced Meritaten. According to a cuneiform tablet, however, it was pronounced Mayati. A fragment of a cuneiform
vocabulary used for teaching the Egyptian language to a Syrian
shows that the common Egyptian word for a unit of weight of
metal, which we transcribe as *deben*, sounded to a foreigner as *ti-
ib-nu*, and the word for an offering table, transcribed as *hetep*,
sounded like *ha-du-pu*. One reason for the gap between spelling
and pronunciation is that the Egyptian language evolved over the
centuries but the Egyptians preferred to keep older spellings of
words. It is possible that there were regional dialects, too, with different pronunciations: one school text records that the confused
babblings of an unsatisfactory colleague were 'like the talk of a
man of the Delta with a man of Elephantine'.

As time passed more and more immigrants and expatriates
from other countries made Egypt their home. Some came
because they wanted a better life; many were brought in as captives. In the Late Period they came as part of the new ruling elites
of Egypt's conquerors. Egypt must have gradually become a
country of many spoken languages. Under the rule of the Persian
kings (525–404 BC) Egyptian gave way to Aramaic as the language
of government. In the last centuries the state language became
Greek. It was said of Queen Cleopatra VII (the last and most
famous queen of that name) that she was the first of her ruling
house to learn Egyptian. Spoken Egyptian may have come to
sound traditional, a mark of provincialism. In the country areas it
nonetheless survived into the Middle Ages, alongside Arabic, and,
written in Greek letters, retains a place in the indigenous Coptic
Christian Church of Egypt.

For religious practices, speech was a vehicle of power. The
Egyptians believed in 'magic', ⟨glyphs⟩ *ḥkꜣ* (*heka*), that could
be summoned through 'utterances' or 'spells', the common
word for which, ⟨glyph⟩ *r* (*ro*), was derived from that for 'mouth'. A
god would be praised for 'his spells of magic'; a lector priest
who read the temple liturgy boasted that he 'knows his spell';
the temple library of Edfu described its holdings as books,
instructions, laws and 'Spells for averting the Evil Eye'. In all

these cases it is likely that, to be most effective, the spells were spoken aloud. The recitation of the sacred liturgy accompanied by the uttering of spells at particular moments would have been another sound of ancient Egypt.

71. BODY

The hieroglyph depicts the udder, with teats, and the tail of a female mammal, perhaps a cow. It writes the word for 'belly' or 'body', especially that of humans, even though the part is based on that of an animal, as is the case with the hieroglyph for 'ear'. The teats make for a more distinctive sign and this presumably explains the choice of a female animal, although Egyptians tended to celebrate the male physique.

Statues of men (especially kings) were mostly intended to stand in temples or tomb chapels, where they received offerings on behalf of the spirit of the statue's owner. They were seen, therefore, only by priests and those privileged to enter the temple. The male body, often with minimal cladding, was normally youthful, its musculature taut and fit. Instead of commemorating events, statues displayed the characteristics for eternal repose. Violent activity was unseemly, and episodes from myth or the battlefield were not suitable subject matter. The faces were mostly benign and confident. From time to time sculptors introduced signs of age and experience, a corpulent body, a lined face. But these are sufficiently uncommon to cause comment today. Women's statues were more passive, slender and modestly clad.

Hunting in the marshlands or deserts was the favoured active pastime for the male elite, but not athletics. In the marshlands, to judge from tomb scenes, men took their whole family along, and they waited patiently while he attempted to spear a fish. Other tomb pictures show sports and games being played by the commoners, as at Beni Hasan, where the tombs of local governors contain film-like sequences of wrestling men included as entertainment for the tomb owner to observe.

Egyptians were exposed to the complexity of their anatomy when they witnessed injuries from warfare or building sites and the butchery of mammals. Moreover, the practice of embalming gave them an opportunity to observe human anatomy regularly. Only a very few papyri remain that deal with aspects of medicine. In keeping with other areas of the Egyptians' technical knowledge, they are not descriptive general treatises but manuals of practical application. One learned by example. Even so, they reveal an impressively detailed knowledge of the body's interior, with an extensive vocabulary to name the parts.

The Edwin Smith Papyrus (named after its first modern owner) is a scribe's copy of a manual on injuries, which instructs on injuries from the head downwards (the papyrus is incomplete and stops in the middle of the 48th case, which deals with the spine). Each case begins with a description of the injury, some examples of which involve exposure of and damage to the brain. The manual would thus have been particularly useful to army doctors prior to the New Kingdom when clubs and axes were common weapons. The majority of cases were said to be treatable, and sensible instructions are provided, but almost a third were judged simply to be beyond treatment. Other papyri, arranged in a less orderly fashion, try to recognize and name the soft linear systems embedded in human flesh, including arteries (which were thought to conduct air rather than blood), ducts for urine and semen, and tendons and muscles. These are united under a separate word, *mtw* (*metu*), and required strengthening and softening through remedies. For a case involving the *metu* of the anus (probably haemorrhoids), for example, the bandaging on of a mixture of ox fat and acacia leaves is recommended.

Generally the medical papyri are written as if the patient is male. One very fragmentary papyrus, however, addresses itself to women's medical conditions, including those connected with pregnancy (see no. 76, 'To be born').

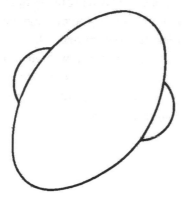

72. PUSTULE

Many conditions that require medical treatment display outward signs: swellings and ulcers, hernias, worms present in faeces, blood in the urine. Swellings seem to be the origin of this curious hieroglyph, which is often used in medical papyri as a determinative sign for morbid conditions. Other conditions, arising from disease and from poor functioning of the body's organs, produce internal pain and fever and the true cause was virtually impossible to detect by ancient Egyptians with the knowledge of the day.

Similar perhaps to the four humours which dominated mediaeval European science, the Egyptians used a word, *whdw* (*wekhedu*), to denote a morbid essence which originated in the bowels (and caused putrefaction in corpses) and could spread through the body by means of the 'channels' (*metu*). But the belief in spiritual forces meant that the Egyptians had a source of illness that must often have seemed as valid as a physical explanation: 'The breath of life enters into the right ear and the breath of death enters into the left ear,' states a medical papyrus. A god or the spirit of a dead person could infect the living with a toxic substance called ⬦𓄿⬦ ꜥꜣ (*a'aa*), or simply have an influence on the course of a sickness.

The prudent course was to adopt a dual approach; to use the remedies from the written sources which had proved effective in the past, while uttering spells to appeal to gods and demons. As an example, the mainly rational Edwin Smith Papyrus, after describing a remedy, continues with a threatening spell: 'What is to be said as a charm over this remedy: Repelled is the enemy that is in the wound! Cast out is the [evil] that is in the blood, the adversary of Horus [i.e. Seth]!'

Medical remedies were drawn from a wide range of substances, from the herbal to the unlikely, and are easily ridiculed today; for example: 'Another [remedy] to cause a child to void an accumulation of urine in his belly: an old book, boiled in oil; his belly is anointed [with it] to regulate his voiding.' Yet the increasing acceptance in modern medicine of the power of placebos, which can prompt the body to produce its own remedies, might suggest that the strange concoctions and dramatic utterances had the same effect and hence were sometimes effective.

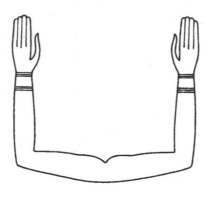

73. KA

The sign is a pair of human arms, from extended fingers to shoulders, bent at the elbows to point upwards. It is used to write the word 'ka', the best translation of which is 'spirit' (but different from no. 53), as compared to the Egyptian word 'ba' which can be translated as 'soul'.

The ancient Egyptians believed their conscious self to be not a single being but to have multiple roles and manifestations to which they gave separate names. A prayer in a tomb illustrates the different elements Egyptians believed made up their being. Amenemhat, a scribe, prays that all these parts of himself will live on in the afterlife: his ka, the memorial tablet at his tomb (through which his name would be kept alive), his ba, his destiny, his life, his 'illumination', his body, his shadow, his place of origin, his upbringing, his personal creator-god (Khnum), 'all his modes of being', each and every one of them described as a 'god'. That a person's whole being should be seen as having so many components shows an awareness of the complexity of personal existence. It is naturally rooted in Egyptian culture and language which we do not share, but our ideas about existence today are still based upon belief rather than upon scientific demonstration, and remain scarcely less mysterious now than in ancient Egyptian times. Theologians pondered over the ka, its power and origin. Where did it come from? Was it indivisible?

The ka is one of the most frequently encountered signs on monuments and was an important manifestation of the self. Prayers written in tomb chapels or on tombstones – which often list the food offerings to be made to a buried Egyptian and specify on which feast days they were to be presented – are addressed not directly to the deceased, but to his or her ka. Close to where the ka was named there was normally a prominent image of the deceased, either a picture or a statue, on which the person making the offering could focus attention.

The ka had an existence separate from the bodily self. Egyptians spoke of a person travelling to or even in the company of his ka at their death. Among the deities who protected the dead were the four sons of Horus and one of them, Imset, could bring your ka to you. Sometimes an important person – occasionally a high official but mostly kings – was said to have several kas. A temple could be said to possess a ka, a not unreasonable quality to apply to a building of such large sombre architecture: the idea that quiet, enclosed spaces are home to a presiding spirit, the *genius loci* of the Roman world, seems to be a deep-seated one.

The presence of the dead could seem very real in ancient Egypt. It was a common experience to enter a chapel in a cemetery and face a statue of the deceased, or sometimes a place, marked by a slot or hole at eye-level, where you knew that a statue had been hidden in a sealed and darkened chamber for protection. In more modest circumstances many must have stood or knelt in front of nothing more than a tiny niche containing a crudely carved or painted flake of stone, and murmured a simple formulaic prayer for offerings while setting down a jug of beer and a loaf of bread for the benefit of the ka of a deceased relative or friend.

Indeed, in the tomb prayers, the deceased sometimes entreated passers-by to enter and recite the offering prayer, promising good fortune in return. For those who could afford it, a ka-priest, ideally the eldest son, was paid to carry out the rite; a charitable foundation would be set up for this purpose. People left letters to the dead at tombs, asking for help with family and personal problems.

The kas of the gods were created by an ultimate creator-god. Indeed, like important people, each deity could have several kas. In some texts the sun-god Ra is credited with 14, each with its own name. Some of the temples at Thebes, for a long time Egypt's ceremonial centre, existed to celebrate the divinity of the Pharaoh. One set of scenes, well preserved in the temples of Amenhetep III at Luxor and in the mortuary temple of Queen Hatshepsut at Deir el-Bahari, portray the Pharaoh's divine conception, and depict the way the body and the ka of the king came into existence together. The ram-headed creator-god Khnum fashions the twin persons of the future king – his real self and his ka – on a potter's wheel. In subsequent scenes the Pharaoh's body and ka, identified by the ka sign above his head, are received by other gods. The temple of Luxor appears to have been designed around an annual Festival of Opet during which the king renewed his divinity through a mystic union between himself and his ka, the latter represented by a separate statue carried in a boat-shaped shrine. At the culmination of the festival the king emerged as foremost of all 'the living kas', a collective term for the unbroken line of past kings. The legitimacy of his rule was in this way placed beyond doubt.

Away from tombs and temples the word 'ka' developed a wider usage in the everyday world. In the New Kingdom, the same pious prayers addressed to an Egyptian's ka appeared on the doorframes of houses. Made from carved and painted limestone these were intended to last beyond the lifetime of the owner. His ka then became a guardian spirit for his descendants. When corresponding by letter, an Egyptian might politely address or refer to the ka of the recipient to preserve a respectful distance between the two parties. A modern polite translation of 'by the ka of Pharaoh' might be 'by the good grace of Pharaoh'. By the first millennium BC the term had become simply a synonym for a person's name when it was 'called out' or 'remembered' in a religious context.

When, in the profane setting of a banquet scene in a tomb, a servant encourages a woman to drink wine to excess with the words 'for your ka', we seem to have travelled even further, to the colourful phrases of toasts, where exact meaning is lost. In another form of extravagant speech, the oath, an Egyptian could swear 'by the ka of' one of the gods, as when a scribe declares of a piece of his own writing: 'As the ka of Thoth endures, I did it all by myself.' It is impossible to know if this embellishment impressed readers or listeners more than if he had simply sworn in the name of the god directly.

A striking use of the word is to be found in a tale of shipwreck where the surviving sailor is cast up on the shore of a fertile island whose only inhabitant, a giant and kindly serpent, reveals that the place is only an 'island of the ka' – a modern equivalent would be 'island of the imagination' or perhaps 'magic island'.

74. BA

The Egyptian's word for 'soul', 'ba', is denoted by a human-headed bird. The soul was conceived as a living force, and often imagined in prayers at the tomb as several different birds in flight (see no. 77, 'To come into existence'). The hieroglyph's human head suggests that this aspect of the inner self most closely resembled the outward, physical person.

The ba was to be nurtured by its owner during a lifetime. 'The wise feeds his ba with what endures [that is, wisdom], so that it is happy with him on earth,' said the sage Ptahhetep; 'A man should do what profits his ba,' a wise king counselled his son Merikara. The ba's future existence was tied to the place and style of life of its owner: 'So also the ba goes to the place it knows, and strays not from its former path.' The lesson presumably was that the future life of one's soul was determined by the life one had lived on earth. The loss of one's ba represented unconsciousness. Sinuhe, the exile pardoned by his king, reacts to his first royal audience:

'I was like a man seized by darkness. My ba had gone, my limbs trembled; my heart was not in my body; I did not know life from death.'

One of the most remarkable texts to have survived from ancient Egypt is a dialogue between a man and his soul, written during the Middle Kingdom. The man feels alienated within a friendless, selfish society and longs for the happy release of death. His ba has no sympathy and urges the man to make the best of being alive, contrasting this with the bleakness of death, when the man 'will not rise up to see the sun', but will be reduced in time to a status in the afterlife similar to that of poor people who died in the open on the riverbank. In the end the man praises death with such sweet poetry that his ba feels soothed and promises to remain with him after death when they will both dwell together. For a person to experience the afterlife, the ba was essential, as expressed in this prayer for the dead: 'Come forth as a living ba, see the sun-disc at dawn, come and go in the sacred cemetery without one's ba being held back from the necropolis.'

Several of the more powerful gods, such as Ra and Shu, had a soul like the human ba, referred to in a prayer for a commoner: 'May your ba alight in heaven behind the ba of Ra; may your shadow walk upon earth.' Gods could actually possess multiple souls. A hymn to Khnum describes him as the ba, or 'manifestation', of several of the great gods, of Ra, Shu, Osiris and Geb. Certain places of ancient sanctity had 'souls': the cities of Heliopolis and Hermopolis, each centres of religious learning; Pe (Buto in the western delta); and Nekhen (Hierakonpolis in Upper Egypt), which had been prominent before the beginning of the dynasties.

'Ba' used in the plural developed a special meaning; it implied the 'manifestation' of a god or of the king, which induced a surge of terror in a guilty person. A woman of Deir el-Medina, accused of having stolen a chisel, swears an oath of denial, invoking the god Amun and the king 'whose manifestation [or 'souls'] is worse than death'. She was accused by another woman, who had spontaneously suffered her own 'manifestation of god', evidently a pang of guilt. On other occasions a transgression against a god brought about a wish to atone. A workman named Huy had falsely sworn an oath in the name of the god Thoth in connection with an accusation levelled against him. When Huy subsequently encountered the god's 'manifestation' he confessed and recorded the moment on a carved stone probably set up in one of the village chapels.

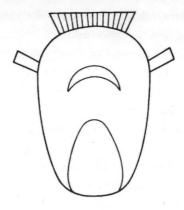

75. HEART

Although the Egyptians made no connection between the heart and blood they linked the heart and the pulse, and developed a series of diagnoses for heart conditions. One of the medical papyri summarizes the medical knowledge:

> There are vessels in him to all his limbs. As to these: If any doctor, any priest of Sekhmet, or any magician places his two hands or his fingers on the head, on the back of the head, on the hands, on the place of the heart, on the two arms or on each of the two legs, he examines the heart because of its vessels to all his limbs. It speaks from the vessels of all the limbs.

The Egyptians used terms for a malfunctioning heart such as 'weary', 'hot', 'kneeling', 'flooded' and 'dancing'. Believing that arteries carried air and connected up with the digestive areas, it seems not illogical that their word for the stomach was 'the heart's mouth'.

There were two words for heart, $\bar{1}$ *ib* (*ib*) and $\otimes$ $\overline{\overline{\triangle}}$ *ḥȝty* (*haty*), which were used interchangeably in the medical papyri, although some nuances existed. In other sources, $\bar{1}$ *ib* was the preferred term for the heart as the seat of thoughts and emotions, and is sometimes translated as 'mind', 'opinion' or 'will'.

A theological text describes the primacy of the heart in the phenomenon of life, created in time past by the god Ptah. The thoughts of his heart, uttered by his tongue, summoned up life:

Sight, hearing, breathing: they report to the heart, and it makes every understanding come forth. As to the tongue, it repeats what the heart has devised. Thus all the gods were born and his Ennead [company of nine gods] was completed. For every word of the god came about through what the heart devised and the tongue commanded. Thus all the faculties were made and all the qualities determined . . . Thus life is given to the peaceful, death is given to the criminal. Thus all labour, all crafts are made, the action of the hands, the motion of the legs, the movement of all the limbs, according to this command which is devised by the heart and comes forth on the tongue and creates the performance of every thing. Thus it is said of Ptah: 'He who made all and created the gods.'

The heart was one of several spiritual components of a person, revealing itself particularly at the moment when, after death, it was weighed in the hall of judgement against the symbol of truth (see no. 58, 'Truth' and no. 90, 'Balance'). If guilty of wrongdoing it would weigh heavily, and would reveal the owner's misdeeds. A text composed for the Book of the Dead, wrapped in with a mummy, would guard against the heart's revelations. Written in tiny hieroglyphs on the base of a scarab-shaped amulet of dark stone it would proclaim:

Spell for not allowing the heart of N to create trouble for him in the necropolis. He says: 'O my heart of my mother, my heart of my mother, my heart of different ages: stand not up against me as witness, create no trouble for me as a witness, create no trouble for me amongst the judges. Do not weigh heavy against me in front of the keeper of the scales. You are my spirit [ka] which is in my body, the Khnum (creator-god) who sustains my limbs.'

With this safeguard the heart was returned to the body after mummification.

In contrast to this somewhat pragmatic (and some might say cynical) approach is the advice given by a king to his son to relish the rewards of good deeds: 'When a man remains over after death, his deeds are set beside him as treasure, and being yonder lasts forever . . . He who reaches them [the judges] without having done wrong will exist there like a god, free-striding like the lords of eternity.'

76. TO BE BORN

Despite beliefs that human lives originated from clay on a potter's wheel by the creator-god Khnum, or were the 'tears' of god (this based on a pun between the words for 'tears' and 'mankind'), Egyptians knew that sexual intercourse was the basis of reproduction. In one story a lady is attracted to a blind vagrant found lying amid the reeds and has him brought into her house. 'He slept with her that night and knew her with the knowledge of a man. She conceived a son that night.' Although Egyptian temples relentlessly maintained that the king was born from a union between his mother and the sun-god, secular literature accepted that, in reality, the royal family was no different to any other. A king who lacked a son prayed to the 'gods of his domain'. 'That night he slept with his wife and she [became] pregnant. When she had completed the months of childbearing, a son was born.'

Sources, including the childbirth hieroglyph itself, suggest that women gave birth in a squatting position resting on one or more specially made bricks decorated with protective symbols, often a picture of the deities Bes and Taweret, and pictures or symbols of the goddess Hathor. A description of childbirth is found in a tale of the miraculous birth of triplets, to the wife of a priest of Ra the sun-god, destined to be future kings of Egypt. A group of goddesses are sent out by Ra himself to assist with the delivery, one of them, Meskhenet, having the same name as that given to the birthing bricks. They transform themselves into a troupe of female entertainers, with the creator-god Khnum changing into their porter. They find the father 'standing with his loincloth untied' and eager that they assist his wife:

> Isis placed herself in front of her, Nephthys behind her, and Heket hastened the birth . . . The child slid into her arms, a child of one cubit, strong boned, his limbs overlaid with gold, his headdress of true lapis lazuli. They washed him, having cut his navel cord, and laid him on a pillow of cloth.

The goddesses tell the priest of the successful delivery of the triplets, and he pays them with a sack of barley from which to make beer. Subsequently the wife 'cleansed herself with a cleansing of fourteen days'.

A category of stylized pictures, many from Deir el-Medina and hastily drawn on flakes of limestone, celebrates the events after childbirth. They show the mother nursing her child on a stool or on or beside a wooden bed, decorated with protective symbols including the god Bes, a protector of women in childbirth. The stool or bed is beneath a canopy twined with the leafy convolvulus plant, though it is not clear whether this was a room in the house decorated for the occasion or was a place specially constructed for childbirth. Mothers could expect a prolonged period of breastfeeding. The sage Any reminds his reader that: 'When you were born after your months, she was yet yoked [to you], her breast in your mouth for three years.' Some could afford a wet-nurse, a woman with her own baby and the capacity to feed two. A workman at Deir el-Medina named Userhat paid a wet-nurse three necklaces of red jasper, one piece of timber, a basket, an ivory comb, a pair of sandals and a jar of oil for this service (perhaps his wife had died in childbirth).

Pregnancy and childbirth fell under the care of Egyptian 'medicine', a complex mix of rational practice and magic. Surviving papyri contain tests for fertility, for pregnancy and to determine the sex of the unborn child: 'Emmer and barley, [put] like dates and sand in two bags, the lady should moisten with her urine every day. If both sprout, she will bear. If the barley sprouts, it means a boy; if the emmer sprouts, it means a girl. If neither sprouts, she will not bear a child.' They offer remedies for a range of gynaecological problems: for example, when the pubic region is 'very swollen due to giving birth: you should then prepare for her 1 hin [450 millilitres] of new oil, to be soaked into her vagina'. These medical texts recognize – significantly, because the texts were almost certainly written by men – that women do not necessarily want to keep bearing children, and offer contraceptive remedies to halt fertility: 'Beginning of the prescriptions prepared for females to allow a woman to cease conceiving for one year, two years or three years: acacia leaves [or thorns?], carob, dates; grind with 1 hin of honey, spread it on a strip of linen and place it inside her.'

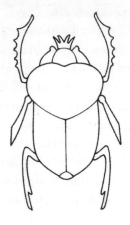

77. TO COME INTO EXISTENCE

The hieroglyph depicts a scarab beetle (*Scarabaeus sacer*), sadly no longer common in Egypt. It stands out from other insects by forming a perfectly spherical ball (about the size of a tennis ball) of mud and dung around its eggs which it can then roll to a safe place. Eventually the eggs hatch and new beetles emerge. The beetle became a vivid metaphor both for the phenomenon of coming into existence, expressed through the verb ☒ *ḫpr* (*kheper*), and the movement of the sun across the sky, the sun itself being regarded as the source of life. The beetle was named 'Becomer' (Khepri), and was considered a manifestation of the sun-god, who 'wearies himself with toil' as he pushes the disc of the sun across the heavens.

The verb, *ḫpr*, was used to describe the emergence of most things: light, darkness, illnesses, persons at the time of their birth, their name. The creator-god 'came into existence through his own agency' out of the primaeval water, 'without a mother', at the

beginning of time (see no. 52, 'Primaeval time'). Although the
Egyptians did not develop the concept further, their use of a
derived word, meaning 'forms', ⟨hieroglyphs⟩ *ḫprw* (*kheperu*), suggests they saw even gradual subsequent change as a series of
replacements of old forms by new. An Egyptian described the
course of growing up as 'making my forms', and the process
could continue until death. At the time of final judgement there
was a danger that testimony of ill conduct would be given by the
heart 'of my different forms' (that is, stages of life or ages). The
Egyptians also maintained a limited belief that gods, kings and the
spirits of the dead could change themselves into different 'forms'.
A prayer for the mayor of El-Kab, Paheri, envisages that his 'living
soul' [ba] will 'assume the form of a phoenix, swallow, falcon, or
heron, as you please'.

78. CHILD

It is easy to assume, though we have no actual proof, that ancient Egypt had a very high infant mortality rate. We have very little information on family size. A fragment of a papyrus census of the workmen's village of Deir el-Medina names no more than two or three children in any one house. On the other hand, a widow of the same place, named Naunakht, in drawing up her will, disposed of her property among her eight children, who had clearly survived infancy. A reconstruction of population size assumes that a gradual increase took place over the entire period of ancient Egyptian civilization – from around one million in the 1st Dynasty to perhaps three million at the time of the Roman conquest – but there was no population 'explosion', such as has happened in modern times. Immigration accounted for some of the increase, but it is also likely that the rate of reproduction was only a little above that of simple replacement.

The hieroglyph for 'child' is the outline of a boy sitting on an adult's lap with a finger held to his mouth. It was customary for boys to have their heads shaved except for a long twisted sidelock of hair (which the hieroglyph omits). Several objects have been found in excavations in Egypt, both in tombs and among houses, which look like children's toys: balls made from wood or segments of leather sewn together and stuffed with dried grass or barley husks; 'tops' made from wood and faience (a bright-blue glazed substance); human and animal figurines, some with movable parts (for example, a wooden feline whose hinged jaw can be moved up and down by means of a piece of string taken up through a hole in the head – like a few others it is the product of skilled craftsmanship). In calling them toys we tend to assume that they are for children but this is by no means definite.

Several tomb scenes of the Old and Middle Kingdoms show boys playing games in groups. They are naked and sometimes wear the child's sidelock of hair. They climb onto each other's shoulders; they jump over the outstretched arms of seated companions. In a game entitled 'building the wine arbour' a pair of boys stand and, with arms extended, grasp the wrists of another pair of boys who lean backwards and allow themselves to be spun around. From the same period and later come pictures of groups of girls who dance and juggle balls. They might have continued these performances into adulthood, sometimes dancing on religious occasions. One of the monuments celebrating Queen Hatshepsut's coronation is a red quartzite shrine at Karnak temple. It shows a procession of girls or women somersaulting backwards, accompanied by musicians playing harps and sistra (see no. 67, 'Sistrum').

An Egyptian childhood did not exclude responsibilities that today we might consider belong to adulthood. The tomb biography of a senior priest, Bakenkhensu of the time of Rameses II, records that after passing four years as a child, for the next eleven years as a youth he was a trainee stablemaster in one of the royal stables. During this time he attended a school attached to the temple of Mut. He became a priest and rose through the senior ranks of the priesthood of Amun over a period of 70 years. He was presumably close to 90 when he died.

An important mark of the transition from boy to man was circumcision, although evidence from mummies shows that not all families chose to circumcise their children. One man's tombstone epitaph records that he had 'achieved office before he was circumcised'. The statement by another man that he had been circumcised along with 120 others suggests that it was made into a ceremony for the entire age-group of the community and not centred on the family.

Egypt's most famous child is Tutankhamun, about 18 years old when he died but about eight when he became king, probably not far short of the age at which children generally began to accept the responsibilities of adulthood. The large collection of textiles from his tomb include loincloths and tunics which, to judge from their dimensions, were made for him early in his reign (although the designs are the same as those for adults). The same must be true for his small ebony chair, only 39 centimetres deep and 71 centimetres high to the top of the back. Probably a son of King Akhenaten and married to one of his half-sisters (Ankhsenpaaten), but probably not the next in line of succession, Tutankhamun found himself heir to Akhenaten's troubled legacy of religious reform. It was he who rejected his father's monotheism and re-opened the temples to the old gods, whether from personal conviction or from the influence of others we do not know.

79. OLD MAN

Half of ancient Egyptians born at any one time would be dead by around the age of 30, from disease or warfare. But those possessing a strong constitution could expect to reach a respectable age. Senior priest Bakenkhensu must have lived to around 90 (and clearly faced no compulsory retirement). His king, Rameses II, ruled for 67 years.

A tale about the magician Djedi gives us a picture of a venerable old man. A visiting prince finds Djedi 'lying on a mat in the courtyard of his house, one servant beside him anointing him, another rubbing his feet'. The prince greets him with the words: 'Your condition is like that of one who is ageless; for old age is the time for death, enwrapping and burial. [You are] one who sleeps till daytime free of illness, without wheezing.' As the story develops we find that, presumably on account of the veneration that accompanies his extreme age, he attracts no wrath from the king when he refuses to demonstrate, using a living human captive, his ability to join severed heads to bodies and bring them alive again. Djedi is said to be 110 years old at the time. This age recurs in Egyptian literature as an ideal to hope for: 'May he [the god Atum] vouchsafe you 110 years upon earth, your body whole, growing old with a contented heart.'

Men (the sources here say nothing of women) desired not only to retain their health but also to attain a level of respect: 'I reached the old age of an honoured man, being daily in the favour of His Majesty, fed from the table of the king.' They hoped to see their sons settled in good positions: 'I was allowed to reach old age, with all my children holding office in the palace.'

In the hieroglyph a man leans on a staff. Many examples of staffs have survived from tombs: straight, naturally sinuous, with curved, forked and flanged ends made by leaving a small amount of the original parent branch or trunk projecting upwards and downwards at an angle. Staffs could have bronze inlays, bear the owner's name, and, if they belonged to a king, be carved and sheathed in gold. A court lady, Senebtisi, was buried with six staffs lying beside her in her coffin, and others in a special long box. Tutankhamun, despite his youth, was left with 130 sticks and staffs, perhaps showing that a staff was not exclusively bestowed in old age.

Ideally a man would have a dutiful son to succeed him in whatever office he held and to look after him. The son would be 'a staff of old age', as the Egyptians put it, including in the legal texts which transferred an office from father to son with the Pharaoh's permission. A particular office, of governor of a province or of priest, for example, might remain in the same family for several generations. In the late New Kingdom one Theban family held many of the most senior offices in the Amun priesthood for almost two centuries, until military families broke the succession and took over.

Not all lived up to the family ideal. The widow Naunakht discriminated in her will between her eight children, five of whom had been kind to her in her old age and who would therefore inherit her property, and the three others (a man and two women) who had not helped her and who would receive nothing of hers, although they were entitled to receive a share of their father's contribution to the marriage property.

80. OFFICIAL

In this hieroglyph the man holds a staff but, unlike the hieroglyph for 'old man' (see no. 79), he stands upright, and in his other hand holds a piece of folded cloth, which, like the staff, was a mark of status. Status in ancient Egypt was primarily measured by the number of titles one had, with the grand officials of the later Old Kingdom collecting the most. The vizier Mereruka, in his tomb at Sakkara, managed almost a hundred: they included a mixture of jobs actually done at some point in his career and of titles bestowed as a mark of honour, probably in each case bringing with them an income or pension. An Egyptian inscribed his titles in his tomb, on his statue in the local temple, and around the stone doorframe to his house. He sealed documents with a ring or other kind of stamp which, in the space available, wrote his name and principal title in small hieroglyphs.

A common title stated that you were in charge of something, either an institution (for example, a granary) or a body of people (for example, young recruits). This title, when translated literally – 'one who is in the mouth' – sounds like colourful slang, and was often written playfully using a hieroglyphic sign for a tongue, Γ. The convention is to translate the title as 'overseer', although in certain jobs better alternatives suggest themselves: 'steward' for 'overseer of a house' (rich men would normally have employed at least one), 'senior officer' or even 'general' for 'overseer of the army', and 'mayor' for 'overseer of the city'.

Men with ambition in what was ancient Egypt's civil service needed versatility backed by broad practical knowledge. A scribal school practice exercise written, in a tone of mockery, by an official named Hori about a colleague named Amenemope shows what an official should be ready for at short notice: calculating the number of bricks needed for a giant construction ramp; estimating the number of men needed to drag an obelisk from the quarries; how to set upright a colossal statue, using sand-filled chambers at the end of a ramp. Suddenly the story shifts from engineering and logistical works in Egypt to foreign campaigning: Amenemope finds himself sent on a military campaign to Syria. It is his job to supply the food, and also to guide the army by means of his detailed knowledge of local geography: 'As for the River Jordan, how can it be crossed?' 'How many leagues' march is it to Gaza?' The Egyptian ethos promoted competence; their style of education created an elite who looked for rewards for doing jobs well. This culture helps explain the success of ancient Egypt's civilization.

The Egyptians promoted men on merit, and on loyalty to the regime. Some officials made a point of recording their lowly origin. Akhenaten's fanbearer, named May, put it plainly: 'I was a poor man on both my father's and my mother's side; but the ruler built me up, he advanced me, he fed me by means of his ka when I was without property. He enabled me to acquire people in numbers', the last sentence a reference to dependants, including slaves. The sage Ptahhetep offers advice to the young man entering the service of someone like this: 'Do not recall if he once was poor; do not be arrogant toward him for knowing his former state.

Respect him for what has accrued to him, for wealth does not come by itself.' In reality, promotion by merit was countered by the deep-seated wish of men to pass their office to their sons.

Although offices could be sold or transferred by legal deed, generally appointment and promotion rested with the king and was signalled through written commands and solemn ceremony. Nebnefer records how his promotion to his father's post in the granary of Amun's temple at Thebes as 'keeper of measurements' – not a very elevated office – began with a high official delivering an authorizing letter from the king, who was at Memphis, to the high-priest of Amun at Thebes, who in turn formed a six-man committee of his most senior colleagues to approve the post, so that Nebnefer could feel that his promotion came with the full weight of royal approval.

Some titles were closed to those rising only by their own merits, particularly land-owning titles. These belonged to local governors, who were also normally the chief priests of local temples. They formed local dynasties, their authority depending upon their ownership of land and traditions of local deference. These must be the men who one king had in mind when giving to his successor (named Merikara) the advice to place more trust in rich men rather than poor, for the latter, through envy, will be more inclined to accept bribes.

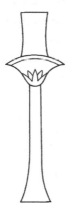

81. SCEPTRE OF POWER

The hieroglyph depicts a sceptre of office with a cylindrical handle
ending in a lotus, above which rises a flat panel with slightly con-
cave sides. We do not know how it originated. It is used in writing
several words for control, the most common being ⌐𝔏 ⎮ *sḫm*
(*sekhem*), 'power'.

In statues and pictures, Pharaohs often hold symbols of power
in their hands. Sometimes two ornamental symbols of office, the
flail and the crook – like a shepherd's – are held across the
Pharaoh's chest. Another symbol of authority was a folded piece
of cloth, held in the hand by officials as well as by kings. The
sekhem sceptre of power was also grasped by the Pharaoh and
high officials, and must have been particularly satisfying to hold
since it actually wrote the word for 'power'. Tutankhamun was
buried with a *sekhem* sceptre in his tomb, made from wood and
with decorated gold sheeting covering the flat panel.

Through the addition of a pair of decorative eyes at the base of the panel, the *sekhem* sceptre came to be seen as a manifestation of the power of a god. It became a cult image, revered in temples. In one example, in the temple of Seti I at Abydos, the accompanying text demonstrates one of those sideways associations that recur in Egyptian thinking. It is labelled, 'Thoth, mighty one of the gods', and so represents the power of Thoth even though it carries no added detail that we can associate with that god. Were it not for the label we would not make the association.

82. SCRIBAL KIT

The sign is a flat palette on which black and red ink could be mixed, a narrow solid tube to contain a reed pen, and a little bag for powdered pigments. It principally serves as the dominant sign in writing the word 𓏞 sš (*sesh*), 'to write, draw or paint'. From it came the word 𓏞, 'writer', which we invariably translate as 'scribe'. Scribes were from an educated class of people who managed the country. The role of scribe was so honourable that Egyptian statues often depicted a man as a scribe: sitting cross-legged with a papyrus scroll across his lap, his face looking either attentively forward or thoughtfully downwards towards his writing. A famous example, found in the temple of Amun-Ra at Karnak, belongs to Amenhetep son of Hapu, the man responsible for the monumental buildings of Amenhetep III, which included the Colossi of Memnon and the Luxor temple.

Many men bore other administrative titles and we class them all together as 'officials' (see no. 80). Priests, or at least those attached to the major temples, form one category. Presumably all officials began by taking scribal training and were for a time simply 'scribes'. Some kept a version of the title even though they became very senior. Amenhetep son of Hapu continued to call himself a 'royal scribe' and 'scribe of recruits'.

Scribes and their more senior counterparts were invested with an authority over other people, exercised on behalf of the king and the temples. An expedition sent to the quarries in the Wadi Hammamat in the 38th regnal year of King Senusret I (1918 BC) was led by a 'herald' called Ameni. Under him were 80 officials (only eight of whom were identified specifically as scribes) who had charge of roughly 18,660 skilled and unskilled workers (including 30 hunters and a contingent of soldiers), plus a train of millers, brewers and bakers (20 of each together with 50 'butlers'), a ratio of one official to more than 200 men. This is the scale of workforce needed to build a pyramid.

The rate of literacy in ancient Egypt is very hard to determine, and probably slowly increased over time. A modern estimate of full literacy during the Old Kingdom sets it as low as one per cent of the population. At the ancient village of Deir el-Medina, 2000 years later, where more written records covering daily life have survived than from anywhere else in ancient Egypt, literacy must have been far higher, with many of the men and quite a number of the women able to write letters to one another. One of the women was the widow Naunakht, the owner of a remarkable library of papyri built up by several generations of scribes in the village. It contained stories, love songs, magical and medical texts, a complete book of temple ritual, and a manual on how to interpret people's dreams. The survival of papyri on domestic sites in ancient Egypt is extremely rare and it is hard to estimate how much the literate class actually read for entertainment and instruction. If the Naunakht family was not unusual, the literate class collected and read 'books' on a far greater scale than surviving evidence implies.

Scribes were elitist, believing their work of greater value than other professions. These views were passed on to pupils, in the practice texts used to teach boys how to read and write. The various professions in Egyptian society (from peasant to soldier and even chariot officer) are described in the most unfavourable terms. The message is clear. 'Be a scribe, and be spared from soldiering. When you call out the reply comes, "Here I am." You are safe from torments.' Other pieces recount the material benefits, the comfortable villas, the well-stocked farmlands, the life of ease coupled with respect: 'You are the one who sits grandly in your house; your servants answer speedily; beer is poured copiously; all who see you rejoice in good cheer.' 'Be a scribe. Your body will be sleek, your hands will be soft.'

Scribes also felt a vocation: 'By day write with your fingers; recite by night. Befriend the scroll and the palette. It pleases more than wine. Writing for him who knows it is better than all other professions . . . It is worth more than an inheritance in Egypt, than a tomb in the west.' The long-term value came in the preservation of one's name and reputation: 'Man decays, his corpse is dust. All his kin have perished. But a book preserves his memory through the mouth of its reciter. Better is a book than a well-built house, than tomb-chapels in the west.'

The king's palace possessed an elite school for scribes where children could mix 'among the sons of magistrates, with the elite of the Residence'. The high-priest of Amun, Bakenkhensu, attended a school attached to the temple of Mut in Karnak. The workmen's village of Deir el-Medina had its own little school, to judge from the number of scribal exercises found. These exercises, sometimes written on large flakes of limestone rather than on papyrus, included manuals on good behaviour, such as those credited to Ptahhetep and Any, and major literary texts. Another literary institution attached to temples, the 'House of Life', stored and copied papyrus texts concerned with mythology and ritual. A long list of words and place names – an aid to acquiring vocabulary – was compiled by a 'scribe of sacred books in the House of Life' named Amenemope, suggesting that what to us are mundane subjects had a place as well. Akhenaten's city of Tell el-Amarna also possessed a House of Life, a modest building of mud-brick, adjacent to others that seem to have been offices: given Akhenaten's attempts to suppress the old religion, the House of Life is unlikely to have specialized in mythology and ritual. Not far away were found the Amarna Letters, clay tablets written in cuneiform (see no. 56, 'Palace'). Most were diplomatic letters, but some refer to the study of the language and literature of Mesopotamia. Possibly the nearby House of Life was an academy of wider and secular learning.

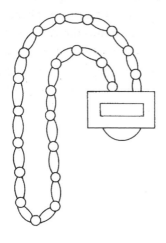

83. CYLINDER SEAL

Seals transferred the authority of officials to the objects under their control; everything from jars of wine to letters, boxes containing linen and the bolts on doors were marked with seals. The earliest seals were little cylinders, mostly of stone, which gave rise to the hieroglyphic sign. It shows a rectangular hollow frame attached to a string of beads (probably to be carried in the hand). Within the frame is a cylinder that rotates on a little spindle. The very first ones were imported from Mesopotamia or Syria before the beginning of the 1st Dynasty and bore Mesopotamian designs carved into the curving surface. When Egyptians began to make their own they replaced these designs with the names of the official, his department and perhaps of the king as well, written in Egyptian hieroglyphs. The impression of the seal was rolled across fine grey clay, which set hard and brittle.

During the Old Kingdom, cylinder seals gradually gave way to seals where the design was carved into a flat base and the impression was made by pressing instead of rolling. In time the design on the rounded backs of stamp seals became standardized to show the image of a scarab beetle. Many Egyptian 'scarabs' are the ancient equivalent of signet rings.

Marking, though not with a seal but by branding, was also extended to humans. Rameses III tell us this in connection with his prisoners-of-war: 'I established their leaders in strongholds bearing my name. I appointed among them chiefs of bowmen, leaders of the tribes, [they being] branded – made as slaves – with the cartouche of my name. Their wives and children were treated similarly.'

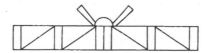

84. PAPYRUS ROLL

The making of papyrus was a distinctive Egyptian industry. It required considerable labour and was manufactured in large quantities. Strips were peeled from the stem and pressed cross-wise in two layers, producing rectangular sheets. These were then joined by narrow overlaps to produce a roll, often made from 20 sheets. The hieroglyph shows a roll of papyrus tied with string in the middle. Over the knot is a lump of mud stamped with a seal. Prices from the New Kingdom show that papyrus was not expensive. A whole roll, which at this period was around four metres long, cost two deben, the price, for example, of a good pair of sandals or two jars of cooking oil. It was common to cut rolls into smaller pieces, to use both sides, and even to erase an older text so that the surface could be re-used.

Writing on papyrus with pen and ink encourages a rapid fluid style of making letters. When writing secular texts on papyrus scribes did not delineate hieroglyphs one by one but used an abbreviated 'long-hand' form of writing, which we call 'hieratic'. The Egyptians did not turn hieratic into calligraphic art, but some scribes developed a bold, even style marked with flourishes.

The word  *mḏꜣt* (*medjat*), 'papyrus roll', can be translated sometimes as 'book', as with 'The Book of Overthrowing Apophis', a collection of spells for the protection of the sun-god Ra from the assaults of the great serpent Apophis and his allies. Although the term 'Book of the Dead' is one of the most familiar from Egyptology, it is not a strict translation of what the Egyptians called it, which was simply 'The coming forth by day'. A cheap copy could be bought in the New Kingdom for the price of a bed or a quality length of textile.

The ancient Egyptian language possessed many relatively abstract words. The Egyptians used the papyrus-roll hieroglyph, , as a determinative for many of these words, treating the sign as a symbol for complicated knowledge which often used or resulted in a written record: 'to know', 'truth (Maat)', 'to barter, exchange', 'to command'.

85. SOLDIER

The sign for soldier shows a kneeling man equipped with bow and arrows. It was added to words meaning both 'army' and 'expedition', of the kind sent out to distant quarries in the desert. Until the New Kingdom, the Egyptians seem not to have maintained a large standing army controlled by the king. Instead, when need arose, men were recruited through a national draft. In the 5th Dynasty a high civil official named Weni was responsible for raising a national army to invade Palestine. He recruited not only through the administrative departments of Egypt but also from the Nubian lands to the south. Although he led the army he bore no military title. At other times he organized quarry expeditions, boat building and the clearing of channels through the rocky obstructions of the Nile at Aswan.

Wealthy men in the provinces maintained their own private armies at times. The governor of a province, Amenemhat, describes in his tomb-biography at Beni Hasan how he led troops of 400 to 600 men from his province for royal expeditions either of conquest in Nubia or to find gold in the desert. The dangers were many and he boasts of the safe return of his men. During a huge expedition, of 9,268 men, sent in the reign of Rameses IV (1153–1147 BC) to quarry stone at a not particularly remote site in the Wadi Hammamat, 900 are said to have died, though the causes are not stated.

Weapons were few and simple in the earlier periods. The bodies of 60 soldiers of the early Middle Kingdom buried in a common grave had been attacked by arrows, knives and clubs, and several had then lain on the ground where they had been pecked and ripped by birds of prey. Spear and arrow heads were still made from chipped stone. Men wore no special body protection or uniform. Although no sources mention this, we have to assume that all men were obliged to learn and practise fighting skills in their town or village.

From the 16th century BC – just before the New Kingdom – the Egyptians faced far more formidably equipped armies on the battlefields of the Near East, and rapidly brought themselves up to date. An early victim was King Sekenenra Taa II of the 17th Dynasty (c. 1560 BC). His mummified head shows wounds from dagger, mace and narrow-bladed axe, some of which pierced his skull. Remarkably x-rays reveal new growth of bone around one of the holes, implying that he must have lived on for a few months at least. The most obvious change in weapons and tactics was the adoption of the chariot (see no. 42), and with it developed an elite class of chariot officer. Bronze weapons proliferated, helmets and scale-armour appeared. Kings built up a standing army divided into regiments, named after gods. Some men volunteered, attracted by the promise of plundered goods and slaves, grants of land at home, and an honourable reputation: 'The reputation of a brave man is in his deeds and will never perish in the land,' declares a Nile warship commander, Ahmose, who had fought in the war that reunited Egypt at the beginning of the New Kingdom. Other young men were snatched from their homes and sent to camps. As the New Kingdom wore on, the ranks were swelled with captured soldiers from the Near East, Libya and the Aegean who now fought for Egypt. Later still came Greek mercenaries. Egyptian society changed profoundly. Officers and soldiers were to be found everywhere. Generals became kings. However, although the king was depicted as a war hero, the celebration of battle did not penetrate far into literature. The scribes maintained their disdain for all manual professions, including that of soldiering.

86. CRAFTSMAN

The sign for craftsman depicts the cumbersome tool used to grind out the interiors of stone vases. The vertical shaft was a piece of wood with a natural fork into which a stone grinding-piece could be inserted. The cutting was done by deliberately-added quartz grains which were trapped between the grinder and the stone of the vessel. To help the craftsman maintain the necessary pressure, a pair of stone weights were attached to the handle at the top end. Crafting finely finished stone vases was one of the earliest industries in Egypt, developing well before the 1st Dynasty but declining in scale during the Old Kingdom. Its legacy is found in later words which use this sign: 'to manufacture', 'workshop' and 'craftsman'. The last word applied to all kinds of arts and crafts, from sculpting to building and to the making of chariots, and also figuratively to the skilled use of words.

There were several titles by which sculptors, outline draftsmen and builder-architects identified themselves although the status of artist was not distinctive, unlike in modern European culture. From time to time artists depicted and identified themselves at work in tomb scenes, though this barely counts as a 'signature'. Moreover, they were celebrated not for their specific artistic achievements, but as great men and loyal officials. The Step Pyramid of King Djoser at Sakkara, Egypt's first monument in stone, is an architectural masterpiece of true originality. We can surmise that the great man at Djoser's court named Imhetep (who much later became a god of healing) was responsible, although none of the titles he bore during his life specify his architectural role.

A great masterpiece of Egyptian art, the painted limestone head of Queen Nefertiti, was discovered along with many comparable pieces in a room of a private house at Tell el-Amarna, belonging to a man named Thutmose. Attached to his house was a series of tiny sculptors' workshops arranged around a courtyard. His room of busts might have served as a showroom. Some workshops where statues were made must have belonged to temples and perhaps to the palace. But one way by which loyal subjects could advance their careers and position in society was to pay to have a statue or a chariot or some other fine object made and presented to the king, sometimes on the festival of the New Year. Some of these gifts would be passed on to the temples. It is likely that Thutmose was catering to these sorts of private customers. He and other sculptors working at this time had to follow the new conventions that King Akhenaten had introduced. A chief sculptor named Bak, son of another chief sculptor, states that Akhenaten himself gave him instruction.

One rare insight into craft is found in the tombstone of the sculptor Iritisen of an earlier period. He reveals how the creative process was thought to come from the world of supernatural forces. As the possessor of artistic talent he 'knew the secrets of the god's book, the conducting of ceremonies, all the magic with which I was furnished'.

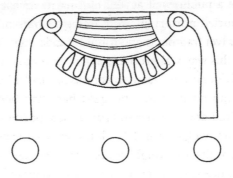

87. GOLD

Around 1360 BC, King Tushratta of the powerful kingdom of Mitanni, in the upper reaches of the Euphrates river, wrote to the King of Egypt, Amenhetep III, begging for gold so he could decorate a memorial to his grandfather. He ended his plea with the words: 'In my brother's country gold is as plentiful as dirt.' This reputation has been backed up in modern times with the discovery of Tutankhamun's tomb and all its gold ornamentation.

Evidence shows that families who were not from the richest section of society could acquire gold. Brave soldiers were given 'gold of valour' by a grateful king, sometimes in the shape of ornamental flies made from gold which could be hung as pendants from a necklace. Officials were rewarded by the king with collars made of gold beads and pendants. The hieroglyphic sign for 'gold' depicts such a collar above a group of three granules (reflecting a common preference for seeing metals derived from granular ore; see no. 3, 'Grain').

The trial records of thieves from the late New Kingdom reveal a black market in gold from thefts from tombs and temples, undertaken with the complicity of junior officials. In a small open space beside a public well at Tell el-Amarna archaeologists discovered a buried pottery jar containing 23 bars of gold and a quantity of silver fragments and roughly made rings. The burial of valuables in this way was probably a fairly common means of safe storage, and does not tell us whether this particular hoard was dishonestly acquired or not. The gold bars had been made by pouring melted-down gold into grooves scooped by the finger in sand. The total weight was 3.375 kilograms, equivalent to 37 of the ancient units of weight called the 'deben' (see no. 90, 'Balance'). Since one deben of gold was roughly equal to 200 deben of bronze, the gold bars were worth around 7,400 bronze deben. With this sum one could purchase a herd of around 70 fully grown cattle and feel affluent. Yet gold was not sufficiently common and cheap for it to be used for the purchase of daily goods. According to the numerous records of buying and selling from the village of Deir el-Medina, although bronze and silver were used to value other things and were sometimes given in exchange for them (as if money), gold never was.

Egypt's gold lay in the hilly, sometimes mountainous desert to the east of Upper Egypt and Nubia. It had to be found, extracted and brought back to Egypt by armed expeditions. In earlier periods, perhaps mainly the Old and Middle Kingdoms, the easiest deposits to access were not veins in the rocky hillsides but the sandy beds of adjacent valleys which had become filled with detritus, including particles of gold naturally eroded from the hillsides. If a supply of water could be found, the gold particles could be washed out by swirling a mixture of sand and water around a shallow pan; or the gold particles could be picked out by hand-sorting on a table. The quantities in any one place might not have been very great. Successful endeavours relied on the supply of abundant cheap labour and the willingness of the prospectors to travel more or less any distance into the desert. This included the deserts of Nubia, home to hostile local populations.

Egyptian goldsmiths crafted impressive artefacts, from the gold-leaf covering of an entire riverboat used to ferry the portable image of the god Amun of Thebes, to exquisitely fine jewellery which employed slender gold wire, tiny gold granules added to a surface for decorative effect, and hollow frames with narrow edges to hold inlays of glaze and semi-precious stones.

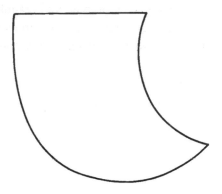

88. BRONZE

Early archaeologists created a scheme for human history based on a threefold development in industrial materials: Stone Age, Bronze Age and Iron Age. The names in a very general way reflect the development of technology, but the periods they describe do not correspond with sharp divisions in the use of materials nor do they represent significant changes in the way that society was organized. Egyptian society in the prehistoric centuries before the 1st Dynasty relied on a substantial and very sophisticated tool-making industry based on flint, even though copper was used over most of this time (see no. 16, 'Sickle'). The Egyptians knew of iron quite early, too, but it remained an exotic and somewhat magical substance until the Persian conquest in the 6th century BC, when iron-working began as an industry. But the gradual replacement of bronze by iron did not herald other kinds of change in society.

The desert regions accessible from the Nile valley, including the southern Sinai peninsula, contain deposits of metals, including copper, iron, and tin on a limited scale. The advantage of copper over iron is that it can be smelted out from its ore and then subsequently cast or beaten into manufactured objects with the use of relatively low temperatures. The hieroglyph depicts a simple pottery crucible in which metal ore was smelted. When written out fully, the granular hieroglyph is added, thus ⟨⟩. (see no. 3, 'Grain').

The addition of tin (the essential ingredient to convert copper to bronze) improves workability and increases the hardness of the product and the potential sharpness of edges. The replacement of copper by bronze proceeded quite slowly in Egypt but was largely complete by the New Kingdom. Modern methods of analysis when applied to ancient Egyptian metal work suggest that Egyptian metal smiths had a sensitive understanding of their craft and controlled mixtures and procedures to produce a particular degree of hardness.

Copper and bronze found widespread use, in axes (as tools and weapons), needles and chisels, as nails for wooden joinery, as scale-plates to make armour in the New Kingdom, as sheeting to cover statues, as domestic utensils, and to fashion into vessels which would hold water much better than pottery versions. In any form, even scrap pieces, copper and bronze held their value because they were a basic unit of exchange, weighed out in deben units. People were careful not to discard metal objects.

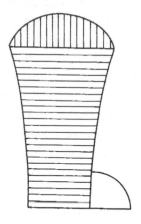

89. POTTER'S KILN

It is disconcerting to walk across an ancient Egyptian town site, for all the time one is crunching ancient pieces of pottery under foot, it is that plentiful. Egypt has abundant clays, from the Nile mud and from deposits in the desert. In the prehistoric periods pottery was sufficiently valued for broken vessels to be repaired, by drilling holes on either side of the break and binding the sherds together. This was also the time when potters added painted decoration to their products. Both traditions died as society became richer during the 1st Dynasty. Thereafter pottery was a cheap utilitarian product that could be easily discarded.

Pottery bowls and cups were used in households as tableware, although we have to assume that richer people also used vessels of metal, including some made of gold in the case of royalty. Pottery vessels with deep bodies and narrower necks were for transporting and storing a wide range of commodities, from water, wine and honey, to incense, joints of meat and cooking oil. Contents were sometimes written on the outside. In the New Kingdom the Egyptians adopted as the standard storage jar a tall two-handled vessel with a pointed base, copied from pottery developed in Palestine and Syria. It was widely transported around the eastern Mediterranean in little trading ships. Two wrecks of these ships have been discovered off the southern coast of Turkey with their cargoes lying on the sea bed, numerous two-handled storage jars among them.

Egyptian pottery was made with skill even though the technology was simple. The potter's wheel was used widely only in the late Old Kingdom, and even then remained a low turntable rotated by hand either by the potter or an assistant squatting on the ground. The hieroglyph which writes the word 'kiln' depicts a simple construction: a tall brick cylinder about two metres in diameter above a circular pit which held the fire. A pierced floor of clay bars kept the stacked vessels separate from the fire beneath, which drew its air supply from a single hole at ground level. A good part of a household's pottery needs were met locally, with only the more robust storage vessels purchased from distant, specialized producers.

90. BALANCE

Many ancient pictures exist of the balances used to weigh items. They were made with an upright post supporting a horizontal beam, pivoted in the middle. From each end hung a shallow metal pan. A plumb-bob separately suspended in the middle helped to ensure that the balance was set upright. To encourage a sense of responsibility a baboon figure, representing the god Thoth, was placed on top. The outline of a balance provides the hieroglyphic determinative to the word ⳡ *mḫȝt* (*mekhat*), 'balance', itself derived from the word *ḫȝỉ* (*khai*), 'to measure'. In everyday transactions a smaller version was used which dispensed with the central post, the owner simply holding the horizontal beam suspended by a short piece of cord.

The balance measured the weight of items against a system of weights based on the deben, which we know is approximately 91 grams, made up of ten smaller units called 'kité'. The reference weights were stones shaped like little cakes, or sometimes carved in more fanciful shapes such as a recumbent ox. The responsibility for ensuring that all deben weights were uniform probably lay with temple staff.

Only certain commodities are suited to weighing; in ancient Egypt most obviously the metals copper, bronze, silver and gold. Evidence from the later New Kingdom points to an informal conversion ratio of silver to bronze of 1:100, and of gold to silver of 2:1. No one weighed grain; it was far too bulky. Instead grain was reckoned by volume, using a scoop of standard size, the 'hekat', and its larger multiple of 16, the 'khar', equivalent to 76.88 litres. From constant practice the Egyptians were able to express the value of a particular measure of, say, grain as being worth so many deben of bronze. Figures from the later New Kingdom show that one khar of wheat or barley was worth two deben of bronze.

As far as we can tell no one needed to keep lists of such equivalences. It was second nature to know that a basket had the value of one deben of bronze or half a khar of grain. This provided the basis for buying and selling in which both parties agreed on the overall value of the transaction, even though the buyer might pay with a mixture of things. We have a receipt which records that a policeman bought an ox from a workman, and paid for it with a jar of fat worth 30 deben, two linen pieces worth ten deben, scraps of bronze weighing (and thus worth) five deben, and 10 hin (the hin being 0.48 litres) of vegetable oil worth five deben. The total came to 50 deben of bronze, the agreed price of the ox.

In the modern world we are used to valuing everything in units of money, the basis of which is faith in a promise extended by banks that the same value will continue to be honoured wherever it is presented. The Egyptian system was based upon real commodities which people could see and touch, economic stability coming from surpluses held in reserve by the palace and especially by the temples.

The balance became a symbol of equilibrium. The city of Memphis was the 'balance of the two lands'. It lay mid-way between Upper and Lower Egypt and was the place where the final reconciliation after judgement took place between the quarrelling gods Horus and Seth. More commonly the equilibrium referred to impartiality on the part of officials, especially those who judged between two claimants and who could metaphorically call themselves 'balance keeper'. In a tale a poor countryman on his way to market is wrongly arrested but turns out to possess the gift of eloquence. With this he attacks the way that those responsible for justice are harsh to the poor. One of his metaphors is the balance: 'Does the hand-balance deflect? Does the stand-balance tilt? Does Thoth show favour so that you (the high official) may do wrong? Be the equal of these three.' The ultimate balance was the one that a person faced when they were led into the hall of judgement after death (see no. 58, 'Truth').

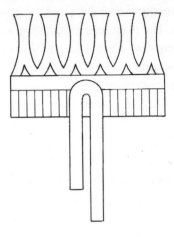

91. CLOTH

The hieroglyph depicts a folded length of cloth combined with a horizontal length of fringe with knotted threads. The example shown here is unusually detailed.

The making of cloth was one of the major industries of ancient Egypt, probably carried out in most households rather than in separate factories. Cloth was used for clothing, sacking, sails and awnings. It was normal in ancient Egypt to produce an excess which went into store, perhaps into a household's wooden chests, where it represented wealth and could be used as a means of exchange on market day.

Today, filmgoers will have an idea that ancient Egyptian men dressed in short kilts, wearing on their heads a piece of striped cloth folded to leave flat lappets on either side of the face. This attire is based on statues of kings and probably bears little relation to reality. Textiles found in Egyptian tombs suggest triangular loincloths were worn either as an undergarment or perhaps by labourers as their sole clothing, and over this wide, loose, sleeveless tunics, and untailored rectangular lengths. Mostly clothing was undecorated except for long fringes down at least two sides of each plain length. The plain lengths served a variety of purposes, depending on their size. They could be tied around the waist to gather in the loose tunic, or wrapped around the body rather like a Roman toga. All securing was by knots and tucks, rather than by pins or brooches. The greatest development of tailoring seems to have taken place in the Old Kingdom, from which period several shaped and stitched women's dresses with bodices have survived.

The style of wearing the wrap-arounds varied from period to period, and of course between men and women. In general Egyptian dress would have had more of a loosely bundled appearance than one expects from looking at statues and tomb paintings. Linen famously takes creases, and this would have contributed to the general appearance of Egyptians, especially towards the end of the day. Statues of the official class from the New Kingdom dress the owners, male and female, in heavier costumes which appear to be elaborately pleated. Some examples of closely set accordion pleats in pieces of linen have survived, but on the statues it is possible that the artist is rendering into a tidy form the natural creasing of linen.

Laundering was a widespread occupation, to some extent done by professionals. To judge from ancient tomb pictures, and models of laundrymen in tombs, it involved much beating of the linen with wooden clubs and tight wrangling to expel the water, either by a pair of men twisting the piece of cloth in opposite directions, or a single man twisting it against a wooden anchoring post. Linen fibres are particularly tough, and rough treatment of this kind renders them softer and more supple. It helps first to rub in a cleansing agent. The Egyptians are mostly likely to have used natron (see no. 3, 'Grain').

Egyptians had a strong preference for plain white cloth, although there were exceptions. Statuettes of servant girls from the tomb of Meketra of the early Middle Kingdom, for example, depict long dresses with coloured patterns. Yet amongst the several hundred items from Tutankhamun's tomb (including about 145 loincloths) very few were decorated.

Written sources speak often of linen, and the numerous finds of textiles in Egyptian tombs almost exclusively comprise linen pieces. We find little evidence of woollen garments, despite the Egyptians owning and farming sheep. Not a single item in Tutankhamun's tomb was made from wool. Among 5000 small cloth fragments excavated at Tell el-Amarna, only 48 (about one per cent) were of wool (some from goats rather than sheep). Yet winter nights are cold in Egypt, and sometimes chill winds can blow during the day. It is hard to believe that the warmth of wool was not appreciated and taken advantage of. Late in Egyptian history the Greek visitor Herodotus noted that while the common people wore woollen garments, it was 'contrary to religious usage to be buried in a woollen garment, or to wear wool in a temple', suggesting that the elite believed wool was unclean.

92. TO BE PURE

The sign is one of a small group of playful hieroglyphs which combine a specific visual act (in this case the pouring of pure water from a jar) with a sign which stands for a dominant letter (in this case the human leg, ∟, which routinely wrote the letter 'b', the last letter of ≋ ▯ w*b* (*wab*), 'to be pure'). Especially during the Old Kingdom, however, artists varied the shapes of individual signs: in the example at the top of the page, a kneeling man substitutes for the leg.

Purity was sought for temples, altars, offerings, clothes, and women after childbirth. Priests should be 'pure of hands' before the gods. The place of embalming was the 'pure place', in one tomb called the 'pure place of wrapping'. The principal means of purification was through washing in water. A not uncommon scene on temple walls shows gods pouring cascades of water over a figure of the king. Unlike Christian baptism the Egyptian ceremony represented an act of regular outward cleansing rather than the passage to a state of grace and entry to a community of believers.

The term 'to purify' could be applied to the restoration of an old temple. In the 13th Dynasty a priest named Amenysenb, of the temple of Osiris at Abydos, received a command from the king to 'purify' the temple. His description of the purification, however, mainly covers cleaning and repairs to the fabric and its wall decoration, for which draughtsmen were supplied who could retouch the painted reliefs and hieroglyphs. For completing this task Amenysenb was rewarded with 'ten heaps of offerings garnished with sweet cakes, and half a young ox'.

'To be pure' gave rise to the principal word for a priest,  *wꜥb* (*wab*), 'pure one'. Not all priests were professionals: at Deir el-Medina, senior workmen ministered to the cult of the dead king Amenhetep I and carried his statue around the village in procession as an honourable spare-time occupation. When on duty priests washed in water deemed to be pure, shaved (including the head; see no. 64, 'Razor'), and swallowed natron (see no. 3, 'Grain'), perhaps dissolved in water. Although their duties were often administrative, some of the priests expressed reverence towards their office: 'I did nothing wrong in his [the god's] domain. I did not neglect what I ought to do in his presence. I trod his ground, bowing and in awe of his dread. I have not been fierce towards his staff, I being [as] a father to them,' wrote the high-priest Bakenkhensu looking back over a lifetime of service to the temple of Amun-Ra at Thebes.

An impure person was barred from sacred spaces including chapels attached to private tombs. Curses in tombs were directed at impurity rather than at robbery. 'As for any man who enters this tomb unclean, I shall seize him by the neck like a bird, and he will be judged for it by the great god,' states Harkhuf in his tomb chapel at Elephantine. Modern visitors to Egyptian tombs who worry about the curse of the Pharaohs should bear this in mind, and prepare themselves with a course of natron ingestion starting ten days beforehand.

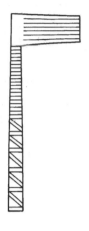

93. TO BE DIVINE

The sign is an upright pole bound with strips of what is perhaps cloth, the ends of which emerge at the top as a group of streamers. It is not an image of anything obviously recognizable, nor related to any religious cult, although the tall flagpoles and streamers that stood against the entrances to Egyptian temples were perhaps modelled on it. The hieroglyph seems to depict something hidden yet designed to catch the attention; something tangible that triggered belief in a hidden world of unearthly power. It wrote the word ꜣ ntry (netjeri), 'to be divine' and hence ꜣ ntr, 'god' and ꜣ ntrt, 'goddess'.

Divinity was found in kings, falcons, temple buildings, sacred mounds, pools of water and, of course, gods and goddesses and their 'spirits' and 'souls'. The Egyptians sometimes interpreted the sensation that lonely desert peaks provoked as a manifestation of the goddess Hathor (see no. 12, 'Tree' and no. 67, 'Sistrum'). The 'Peak of the West' in the cliffs above the necropolis at Thebes was called 'Meret-seger', 'she who loves silence'. For the most part, however, the Egyptians built temples to experience a divine presence.

The central focus of a temple was the statue of the presiding deity (see no. 96, 'Statue'). It normally stood in a shrine at the back of the building, a place of little light, reached by priests through a series of wooden doors which were ritually opened and closed. The statue was kept clean and pure through libations of water, was draped with linen, surrounded with the smell of incense and presented with portions of food and drink as 'offerings'. The spirit of the god that dwelt in the statue also inhabited a portable image, which was paraded outside the temple and seen by the general population. From at least the New Kingdom onwards statues communicated messages by means of an 'oracle' (see no. 97, 'Wonder'). Some were set up in more accessible shrines on the edge of the temple enclosure and could 'hear prayers' from the local populace, though in a carefully managed atmosphere.

Divinity extended to the statues of leading citizens, the provincial governors, mayors and high officials who had local connections. In a small number of cases the cults of these people assumed a status indistinguishable from that of local gods and goddesses: evidence is found on tombstones where Egyptians asked them to intercede to ensure a regular supply of offerings. A vizier buried at the provincial town of Edfu was invoked centuries after his death. More striking still was the governor of Elephantine, Hekaib, who lived in the late Old Kingdom. Two centuries later the local mayors set up a shrine containing his statue in the middle of the town. As the years passed each mayor added his own shrine and statue, as did a few kings. Hekaib's shrine, with its own calendar of festivals, became the principal religious centre for Elephantine for the next two-and-a-half centuries, eclipsing as far as we can see the local cult of Khnum, the creator-god, and his consort, the goddess Satis.

It was not necessary to visit a temple to make contact with the gods. Their blessings could be invoked in private letters, and their presence could be felt in lonely settings. The Egyptian hero

Sinuhe, in exile in Palestine, makes the appeal: 'Whichever god decreed this flight, have mercy, bring me home!' When trouble arose many avenues were open for assistance: places set aside at the local shrine, a doctor or like person who had knowledge of demons good and bad, and one's own dead relatives at their tombs (one could deposit there a letter addressed to the dead asking for or even demanding assistance).

Yet it would be a mistake to think that the Egyptians were more religious than other peoples. The awe towards the divine that they felt in special places did not necessarily persist in familiar surroundings. It was then safe to imagine the gods as fallible, and even to ridicule them. A long and beautifully written papyrus found in the private library of the widow Naunakht at Deir el-Medina retells the conflict between Horus and Seth as a burlesque in which even the greatest of the gods look foolish. Ambivalence extended to the dead. Tomb robbery was as old as careful burial, and songs and poems referred to the difficulty of gaining immortality through tomb-building and to the uncertain fate of the dead. There was a strand in Egyptian thinking that kept religion in perspective.

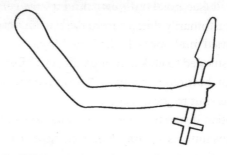

94. SACRED

The hieroglyph shows an arm brandishing what looks like a piece of branch, which itself has been stylized as a particular kind of sceptre. It appears only in a word with the basic meaning 'to clear' or 'to separate'. From this developed the particular nuance of 'sacred', something set aside and segregated from all else. It applied to temple buildings, tracts of land (including the land of Punt which provided incense), the horizon, and the images of kings and gods and their names.

Sacredness wielded considerable power in the Egyptian mind and was taken very seriously. During the festival of Osiris at Abydos, a procession bore the sacred barque of Osiris from the temple across the desert towards his tomb and, along the route, re-enacted an attack by the enemies of Osiris. The tract of ground which the procession crossed was marked out by tall granite slabs (stelae) on which was written a decree for 'the protection of the sacred ground south of Abydos . . . forbidding anyone to trespass upon this sacred ground'. The penalty for disobedience was fierce: 'As for anyone who shall be found within these stelae, except for a priest about his duties, he shall be burnt.'

A secure way of separating the sacred from the profane was by building a wall (see no. 33). Egyptian temples, even when quite small, were customarily shut off from the outside world by a thick wall of sun-dried mud-bricks. In the New Kingdom and later these walls were fashioned to look as though they belonged to a fortress, with a line of battlements along the top parapet. The temple enclosure was shut to the outside world.

The Egyptian distinction between the sacred and the profane was not as absolute as we might expect, however. Although all property of gods was sacred, often that property included all the characteristics of profane daily experience. Temple enclosures could contain storerooms, kitchens, kilns and houses, along with craftsmen, administrators and porters. There were times when the encroachment offended those in charge and purification became necessary. The priest of Sais, Udjahor-resenet, in the time of the Persian occupation of Egypt (525 BC) obtained permission to 'expel all the foreigners [who] dwelled in the temple of Neith, to demolish all their houses and all their unclean things which were in this temple'. Similarly the high-priest of Amun-Ra at Karnak, Menkheperra of the 21st Dynasty, recorded how he had removed the houses of Egyptian people installed in the court of the 'domain of Amun'. In this case we can see that what he did was less thorough than the text implies. Archaeological excavation has revealed that houses lay at this time inside the main temple enclosure and remained there for a long time afterwards. Perhaps what he removed were houses touching the actual stone fabric of the temple. Egyptian religion, despite its impressive scale and elaborate organization, faced inevitable compromises.

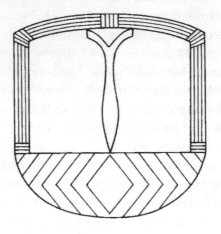

95. FESTIVAL

The Egyptian year was broken by many festivals and religious holidays. The Mayor of El-Kab, Paheri, hoped for offerings in his tomb not only every day, but in particular 'on the monthly feast, the sixth-day feast, the half-monthly feast, the great procession, the rising of [the star] Sirius, the *Wag*-feast, the Thoth-feast, the first-birth feast, the birth of Isis, the procession of Min [and] the procession of the *sem*-priest'. One distinctive festival developed out of the Egyptian calendar. The year was divided into 12 months of 30 days. This left five days over, called 'the five days extra to the year' and formed part of the temple calendar of feasts.

The sources tend to emphasize celebration and indulgence in extra food and drink during festivals. Yet the hieroglyph, in combining the images of a tent-shrine of matting supported by a papyrus column and an alabaster bowl for pure water, sought a more austere association with very traditional buildings and the idea of purity.

Some festivals belonged to only one locality. Particularly

famous was the Festival of Opet which underpinned the primacy
of the city of Thebes in state religion and, for several centuries, the
power of the royal family, which was of Theban origin. It began
during the second month of the Inundation season and lasted for
between 24 and 27 days. For this festival the ornate portable
barques of Amun, Mut and Khensu – the holy family of Thebes –
were conveyed to the temple of Luxor, nearly three kilometres to
the south. The king joined them inside the temple and in a set of
rituals the power of his ka was enhanced through contact with the
kas of his predecessors (see no. 73, 'Ka'). In another festival at
Thebes, the Beautiful Festival of the Valley, the same portable
barques were taken across the Nile to the huge cemetery of
Thebes and to several of the mortuary temples of the kings. It was
an occasion for private families with relatives or ancestors buried in
the Theban hills to make their own journey to the family tomb, to
have a meal there, and to stay overnight. For the workmen of Deir
el-Medina their principal festival was that of their founder, King
Amenhetep I, 'the lord of the village'. One text tells how 'the gang
rejoiced before him for four solid days of drinking together with
their children and their wives'. Extra rations were given out by
the state, and men and women sang and drummed.

Egyptian kings celebrated a long reign with a jubilee festival
called the Sed festival. Images of provincial gods were taken to a
ceremonial site, and the central rite involved the king striding or
running around a course, symbolizing his possession of the two
riverbanks of Egypt. The preference was to celebrate 30 years of
reign, although Amenhetep III followed his Sed festival with two
more, in his 34th and 37th years (the latter the year of his death).
The site of his festivals on the western desert of Thebes survives.
Known as Malkata, it contained a series of palaces, a temple,
storerooms and a complete town. Beside it lay the Birket Habu, an
artificial lake dug in the shape of the letter T. Here, boats imitat-
ing the heavenly boats of the sun-god were launched. It measured
two kilometres long by one kilometre wide and is a monument in
its own right to the scale of resources that kings could direct to
these celebrations.

96. STATUE

Western philosophy since the ancient Greeks has grappled with understanding the essential nature of the world around us. Philosophers have asked what defines an object and gives it its essential form. Egyptians barely formulated such philosophical questions, but they did hold in their minds ideal forms in art and writing and design. In statues personal idiosyncrasies, signs of age and any other departures from the ideal human form were largely suppressed (although there are exceptions; see no. 54, 'King'), to leave an impression of essential humanity, male and female. Primarily a statue's identity was determined by the inscription of a name. Later kings claimed the statues of kings of past ages for themselves simply by carving their name over that of the original owner. Rameses II, in particular, usurped many statues of his predecessors.

The Egyptians believed statues were homes to spirits that existed independently of the statue and were to be addressed as the ka of the statue's owner (see no. 73, 'Ka'). It was said in a major theological document that the creator-god Ptah, after he 'gave birth to the gods', 'made their bodies according to their wishes. Thus the gods entered into their bodies, of every wood, every stone, every clay, every thing that grows upon him in which they came to be.' One word for the creation of a statue was 'giving birth', and a sculptor was 'one who brings birth' (see no. 4, 'Life'). The making of statues of the gods was an especially important act of creation, to the extent that the brief and selective annals of early kings include the creation of several statues as major events in the royal calendar. Once finished, a special set of priests brought the statue to life through the Opening of the Mouth ceremony (performed also over the mummified bodies of the dead before burial), where the mouth of the statue was touched with an adze.

The statues that survive must represent only a very small fraction of the actual ancient output. They are mostly made of stone, but many more would have been made from wood, a substance that deteriorates over time in the damp soil of the Nile floodplain or is consumed by white ants in the desert. Egyptians would have used precious materials for statues of gods, as inlays or, in the case of gold, as a foil overlay, and these are more easily applied to wood. A contemporary description of a statue of Rameses VI shows it to have been made of two kinds of wood, with gold-leaf on the kilt and red faience inlays on the limbs, and provided with an elaborate crown of lapis lazuli 'adorned with serpents of every colour, the uraeus on his head of sixfold alloy inlaid with real stones'.

The larger temples were repositories for many statues. There were statues of the main god and of accompanying deities who were there as if guests in the temple. There were statues of kings, sometimes the same king many times over, sometimes a gallery of royal ancestors. The hieroglyphic determinative for the word 'statue' shows a statue of a king, holding a staff and a mace of office. There were statues of officials and local dignitaries. Each and every one was entitled to receive offerings, carefully orchestrated through a ceremony named 'the reversion of offerings', where offerings circulated around the temple serving each statue in turn. Over time larger or more popular temples would have filled up with statues, and other kinds of material gifts. Those deemed no longer essential were then buried in the temple grounds to make room. The largest find of such a deposit was made late in the 19th century AD, in a courtyard on the north side of the seventh pylon of the temple of Karnak. It contained well over 600 statues of kings and commoners, mostly of the Late Period but extending back to the Old Kingdom, together with around 8000 bronze statuettes, mostly of Osiris.

97. WONDER

Wonder is depicted by a strange sign, hard to interpret. It seems to show a sledge decorated with the head of a jackal, although this was not a feature of sledges known from other evidence. The sledge is bearing a block of some kind. The sign acts as a determinative to the word 𓊪𓂝𓆳𓏤𓏛 *biȝi* (*biyai*), which means 'to wonder, marvel at' and the derivative nouns, 'marvels', 'wonders', 'miracle'.

The word was frequently an overstated degree of admiration: the incense and exotic products of the land of Punt, for example, or the appearance of the king were described as 'wonders'. 'Miracles' were rarer. Around 1990 BC King Menthuhetep IV mounted a huge quarrying expedition to the Wadi Hammamat to bring back large blocks of dark grey stone. The quarrymen had cut a trench around a large rectangular block for the lid of the king's sarcophagus and were preparing to undercut it prior to dragging it off on its long journey to the river. At this delicate moment, a pregnant gazelle approached and gave birth on the block itself. This was recorded in hieroglyphic writing on an adjacent rock face as a 'miracle' which presaged the successful removal of the block. A few days after, another text from the same expedition recorded a second 'miracle'. A sudden rainstorm in the desert hills replenished an ancient well and brought out, perhaps as reflections on its surface, the ghostly forms of soldiers and kings of ancient times.

From the New Kingdom onwards the word 'wonder' took on the special meaning of 'oracle'. Oracles were a direct communication from the statue of a god, either through its motion while being carried or through a message. King Tuthmosis III recorded how, while still a child, he was present in the temple of Amun at Karnak and the statue of the god Amun was steered by the bearers towards him, choosing him to be the next king. To us now, this sounds stage-managed. Egyptian kingship was hereditary. There must often have been several princes, born to different mothers. In the family of Tuthmosis III his aunt, Hatshepsut, was also a successful claimant to the throne, ruling as if she were king for perhaps 15 of the years when Tuthmosis III should have been sole ruler. Although few records survive of the affairs of court, who became the heir to the throne must sometimes have been disputed, as in this case. Using the portable barque-shrine of Amun would have been a way of adding authority to the reigning king's choice of his heir. The senior priests, having been appointed by the king, probably had little influence in the matter.

A well-documented oracle was a portable statue of the dead king Amenhetep I in the village of necropolis workmen at Deir el-Medina. Villagers would consult the statue by presenting a written question – 'Shall I buy this bull?' – to which the statue would give a silent answer by moving forwards or backwards, guided by the men who carried it on their shoulders. The oracle helped solve crimes in the village, by picking out in a similar way one name from a list of the villagers as it was read out. It could, on occasion, deliver a more complicated verdict, read aloud by a living scribe. The priests (who were some of the senior workmen) and scribes were part of the same small village community. The oracle's authority rested upon a communal agreement to accept the verdict delivered, and the divinity of the statue. The sage Amenemope warned against abusing the practice: 'Do not falsify the oracle on papyrus and so harm the plans of god. Do not assume for yourself the power of god as though there were no fate and destiny.'

Occasionally the verdict of an oracle was challenged. In one case a man from western Thebes, accused of theft, refused to accept the decision of his local oracle, tried another and then returned to the first (with a similar indication of his guilt each time). A thrashing finally drew out a confession.

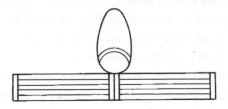

98. OFFERING PLACE

A loaf placed upon a mat is the hieroglyph for 'offering place' or 'altar', ⚱ *ḥtp (hetep)*. Slabs of stone carved with this shape were commonly placed in temples and in tomb-chapels and here the priests or the relatives of the dead would make their offerings. The largest known is a set of four made of alabaster, each measuring four metres, which stood in the 5th Dynasty sun-temple of King Neuserra at Abu Ghurab, in a courtyard where offerings could be presented to the visible sun.

Standard offerings included 'bread and beer, oxen and fowl, alabaster (unguent jars) and linen, all things good and pure on which a god might live'. They were grouped under the heading: 'What comes forth from the voice' (conventionally translated as 'invocation offerings'). The implication is that, although at the outset financial provision was made to supply a cult with real offerings, reciting the list aloud was a sufficient substitute if the supply failed. Some tombs actually invite passers-by to recite the offering prayer, pointing out that 'it is a recital without expense'. In the tombs of the rich and especially in the larger temples the offerings were more extensive and lists specified the different varieties and amounts of each commodity. The offerings for a one-day festival in a Theban temple included 1,034 loaves of ten different shapes and sizes and 90 jugs of beer of two strengths (which together required 15 sacks of grain), one ox, five ducks, three geese, two jars of wine, five baskets of incense, five baskets of fruit, ten bouquets of flowers and ten bunches of flowers. These cases reflected the income of real commodities which properly established cults derived from their estates and which must, in practice, have far exceeded what was contained in the lists. Much of it was used to pay for the services of the priests. All temple income and property, which might include transport boats, could be grouped together as 'god's offerings'.

The word 'offering table' derives from a common word which meant generally 'to be pleased', 'be happy with', and which could become the transitive 'to pacify', 'to make content'. The suggestion is that Egyptians were hoping to bring contentment to their gods through their gifts, as in the statement 'incense of the temple, with which every god is made content'. The same word also meant 'to rest', or 'be at peace', when referring to the dead, and was used to describe the stars and sun when they set.

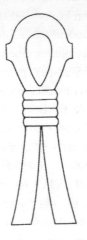

99. PROTECTION

The possibility of chaos was never far away in ancient Egypt. Enemies threatened at the borders, and Egyptians could face sickness and ill luck in their lives. The king sought to protect Egypt by wise and just government (enshrined in the concept of 'Maat'; see no. 58, 'Truth') by performing pious acts for the gods and going to battle to defeat enemies, while the gods constrained the quarrelling divine pair Horus and Seth. At the personal level Egyptians created a world of medico-magical thought and practice to manage dangers, primarily from the intrusion of malevolent forces into their lives. This field of knowledge drew upon conventional Egyptian religion, especially the myths surrounding Ra, Horus and Osiris, as well as medical knowledge. One of the medical papyri illustrates how complementary these two aspects were by pairing 'amulet man' (a word derived from 'protection') with 'doctor', both as professional colleagues and as opponents; for one source of fear was the power of another's magic. So there

were recipes to avert 'the craft of amulets'. An accusation levelled at conspirators against Rameses III suggests they had made
'potions for laming human limbs'. The hieroglyph for protection
shows a simple sheet of bound reeds folded over and tied, such as
was carried by a herdsman as a temporary shelter. The sign writes
the more general word, ⌶ ꜣ (sꜣ), 'protection'.

A collection of spells to protect mother and child illustrates the
unease with which people regarded their world. One of them
reads: 'A protective spell for guarding the limbs, to be recited over
a child when the sunlight rises. You rise, Ra, you rise. Have you
seen the dead who has come against her [the name of the child is
inserted here] to lay a spell on her, laying plans to seize her from
her [the mother's] embrace?' The mother or amulet man would
then speak the words of Ra: 'I shall not give you, I shall not give
your charge to a male or female robber from the West. My hand
is upon you, my seal as your protection!' The seal was a concoc-
tion of 'magic' ingredients: 'a pellet of gold, 40 pellets of bread,
and a carnelian seal stone [bearing] a crocodile and a hand. To be
strung on a strip of fine linen, made into an amulet, placed around
the neck of the child. Good!' In later periods dangers were written
on strips of papyrus, blessed by the gods in a special ceremony,
tightly rolled inside little cylinders, and given to young children.
The dangers included blindness, the collapse of a wall, the evil
eye, magical books, angry gods and goddesses and even gods 'who
seize someone instead of someone [else]'. Outside the walls of the
temples the gods were not to be trusted (see no. 53, 'Spirit').

A special grouping of household gods and potentially dangerous magical creatures could, nonetheless, be enrolled on one's
side. Pictures of some occur lightly incised on curving knife-
shaped 'wands' made of ivory. They include the household deities
Bes and Taweret (manifested as a standing hippopotamus who
guarded mothers and babies), a cat biting a serpent, a crocodile, a
tortoise and a falcon-headed griffin with a winged human head on
its back. A few wands bear the words: 'protection by night and
day', or 'words spoken by these protective figures: we have come
to spread protection over this child'. The points of the knives are

sometimes worn away on one side, suggesting they were used to draw magic circles on the floor, perhaps around where people slept. Presumably a high infant mortality rate made children the special focus of magic and amulets. Among the things that people bought and sold at Deir el-Medina were 'amulets for birth' or 'birth charms', valued between one and three deben, about the price of a pair of sandals.

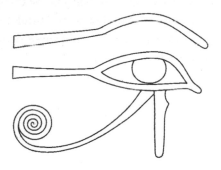

100. WEDJAT (EYE OF WELLBEING)

Egyptian myth describes how, as an episode in their conflict, Seth ripped out the eye of Horus, often conceived as a falcon-god. The god Thoth then reconstituted the mutilated eye and it became known as the 'sound' or 'uninjured' eye. In this myth, Egyptians voiced their fear of destructive forces, and their longing for the triumph that would overcome chaos, a triumph of making something whole, complete. The hieroglyph depicts the eye of Horus (drawn as a human eye) adorned by the plumage that grows below the eye of a falcon. It writes the word 𓂀 wḏꜣt (wedjat), which is derived from a common word, 'to be whole', 'sound' or 'prosperous'. The symbol promoted wellbeing in ancient Egypt, for the living and the dead. The shape was a popular amulet made in faience (the Egyptian blue-glazed compound) or stone, and strung on necklaces or placed among the spread of amulets wrapped into mummies. Laid in rows, they included figures of Anubis, Horus, Isis and

Maat (see no. 58, 'Truth'), scarab beetles (see no. 77, 'To come into existence'), the heart (see no. 75), the Djed-pillar (see no. 59, 'To be stable') and the mason's square, a symbol of correctness. The wedjat-design is found on finger rings and on the thin metal plates that covered the incision in the human body through which the embalmers extracted the internal organs.

The sign developed an unexpected and playful mathematical usage. The separate pieces of the eye when fitted together represented totality: eyebrow, pupil, left and right whites, and the two markings beneath. They became a special set of fractions to measure the standard Egyptian unit of capacity for grain, the hekat (of 4.54 litres). The left side of the white of the eye stood for $\frac{1}{2}$. Each subsequent fraction was a halving of the previous one (the pupil was $\frac{1}{4}$, the brow $\frac{1}{8}$, the right side of the white $\frac{1}{16}$, the spiral design $\frac{1}{32}$ and the bar underneath the pupil $\frac{1}{64}$). We might imagine that, viewed in this way, the idea of wholeness would be best served if all of the fractions when added together came to 1. But their total is actually $\frac{63}{64}$. Egyptian thinking, which now seems so innocent to us, celebrated the world in all its incompleteness and inexplicable variety.

NOTE ON SOURCES

The modern literature on ancient Egypt is extensive and – unlike the case with the sciences – books and specialist periodicals published a century ago remain valuable, often containing the only detailed record of a place or a particular source. Most of the literature is written in English, French or German, and little of it is translated from one language to another. Even less is yet available online; websites still have a peripheral place in Egyptology. The most useful website to what is available online is *www.newton. cam.ac.uk/Egypt/,* a site maintained by the University of Cambridge.

There is no comprehensive study of Egyptian hieroglyphs, sign by sign, detailing all the minor variations and analyzing their meanings and individual histories. The best summary treatment, which contains a numbered catalogue of signs, is Sir Alan Gardiner, *Egyptian Grammar,* third revised edition (Oxford and London 1957). There are several simpler introductions to ancient Egyptian language and hieroglyphs, including Mark Collier and Bill Manley, *How to Read Egyptian Hieroglyphs: A Step-by-Step Guide to Teach Yourself* (London 1998), and Lesley and Roy Adkins, *The Little Book of Egyptian Hieroglyphs* (London 2001). Penelope Wilson, *Sacred Signs: Hieroglyphs in Ancient Egypt* (Oxford 2003) puts hieroglyphic writing into a historical perspective.

A sound history of ancient Egypt is *The Oxford History of Ancient Egypt,* edited by Ian Shaw (Oxford 2000). John Baines and Jaromir Malek's *Atlas of Ancient Egypt* (Oxford 1980) provides detailed maps and a wealth of information on the ancient sites. An excellent and well-illustrated introduction to the remarkable Amarna Period is the exhibition catalogue edited by R.E. Freed, Y.J. Markowitz and S.H. D'Auria, *Pharaohs of the Sun: Akhenaten, Nefertiti, Tutankhamen* (Boston 1999).

Reading translations of Egyptian texts is an unbeatable way of getting to know the ancient Egyptians. Miriam Lichtheim, *Ancient Egyptian Literature: A Book of Readings*, in three volumes (I. The Old and Middle Kingdoms, II. The New Kingdom, III. The Late Period) (Berkeley, Los Angeles and London 1973, 1976, 1980) offers a wide selection, supplemented for the Middle Kingdom by Richard Parkinson, *Voices from Ancient Egypt: An Anthology of Middle Kingdom Writings* (London 1991). A.G. McDowell's *Village Life in Ancient Egypt: Laundry Lists and Love Songs* (Oxford 1999) is an indispensable selection of texts that illustrate the lives of the villagers of Deir el-Medina. Pascal Vernus's *Affairs and Scandals in Ancient Egypt* (Ithaca and London 2003) draws upon papyrus records of trials and accusations dating to the New Kingdom; in John Ray's *Reflections of Osiris: Lives from Ancient Egypt* (London 2001) each chapter is based upon a particular text drawn from a different period of ancient Egyptian history.

Of the many books about ancient Egyptian religion the following cover a diversity of modern approaches: Stephen Quirke, *Ancient Egyptian Religion* (London 1992); Jan Assmann, *The Search for God in Ancient Egypt* (Ithaca and London 2001); Tom Hare, *ReMembering Osiris: Number, Gender and the Word in Ancient Egyptian Representational Systems* (Stanford 1999); R.T. Rundle Clark, *Myth and Symbol in Ancient Egypt* (London and New York 1959, reprinted 1995); and Geraldine Pinch, *Magic in Ancient Egypt* (London 1994). Mark Lehner, *The Complete Pyramids* (London 1997), R.H. Wilkinson, *The Complete Temples of Ancient Egypt* (London 2000) and Salima Ikram and Aidan Dodson, *The Mummy in Ancient Egypt: Equipping the Dead for Eternity* (London 1998) cover those aspects of Egyptian religion where buildings and archaeology make extensive contributions. Again, however, there is no substitute for approaching the texts themselves. Erik Hornung, *Ancient Egyptian*

Books of the Afterlife (Ithaca and London 1999) guides the reader through the main ancient compositions. R.O. Faulkner, *The Ancient Egyptian Book of the Dead* (New York 1972, revised edition London 1985) combines a full translation of the most popular ancient text with fine coloured photographs of one particular example.

Our knowledge of the more pragmatic aspects of ancient Egyptian life and knowledge comes from combining sources of all kinds, including scenes drawn from life which were carved and painted on the walls of Egyptian tombs. Syntheses which have this as their aim are T.G.H. James, *Pharaoh's People: Scenes from Life in Imperial Egypt* (London 1984) and B.J. Kemp, *Ancient Egypt: Anatomy of a Civilization* (London and New York 1989). Studies more closely focused on museum objects are E. Brovarski, S.K. Doll and R.E. Freed (eds.), *Egypt's Golden Age: The Art of Living in the New Kingdom (1558–1085 BC)* (Boston, Mass. 1982) and W.C. Hayes, *The Scepter of Egypt*, 2 vols. (New York 1953, 1959).

The extent and nature of the Egyptians' technical and 'scientific' knowledge can be assessed through John F. Nunn, *Ancient Egyptian Medicine* (London 1996); Otto Neugebauer, *The Exact Sciences in Antiquity* (Princeton 1952) (in which Chapter IV deals with Egyptian mathematics and astronomy); R.A. Parker, *The Calendars of Ancient Egypt* (Chicago 1950); and Corinna Rossi, *Architecture and Mathematics in Ancient Egypt* (Cambridge 2004).

For those wishing to keep up to date with the progress of Egyptology, *Egyptian Archaeology* (the Bulletin of the Egypt Exploration Society, based in London) provides an invaluable service, as does (in a more popular style) the journal *KMT* (San Francisco).

INDEX

Names of hieroglyphs are in **bold** type